DEPARTMENT OF EDUCATION AND SCIENCE

Safety in Practical Studies

Art
Craft, Design and Technology
Home Economics, Dress and Textiles
Music
Rural Science

LONDON   HER MAJESTY'S STATIONERY OFFICE

ii

Designed by HMSO Graphic Design

Printed in the UK for HMSO by Hobbs the Printers of Southampton
(1976/86) Dd739855 C40 7/86 G3379

ISBN 0 11 270305 4

Foreword

The DES Safety Series comprises six booklets dealing with different aspects of the problem of safety in schools and colleges. The booklets, compiled by HM Inspectors, provide advice to teachers on safety education and a general guide to precautions for all who work in the education service.

This present booklet replaces the third in that series. It contains chapters on art, CDT and home economics which are substantially revised. And there are two important chapters on safety in music departments and in rural science departments. New advice given here on the care of animals supersedes that given in *Keeping animals in schools* (HMSO, 1971).

While every effort has been made to give the best advice available after consultation with the many authoritative organisations concerned, no claim is made for comprehensiveness. The advice is not intended for use in connection with any legal proceedings.

Recommendation of a safety measure in this publication does not imply Government commitment to the provision of extra funds. If money is not available for the equipment and facilities necessary to make a particular activity safe, then some other means should be found to provide as nearly as possible the intended educational experience.

Publications on safety in schools and colleges in the DES Safety Series are:

1 *Safety in outdoor pursuits*
2 *Safety in science laboratories*
4 *Safety in physical education*
5 *Safety in further education*
6 *Safety at school: general advice*

The Department of Education and Science issues an occasional bulletin adding to and amending when necessary the advice given in these booklets.

Contents

1 Introduction

1.1   The ever-increasing number of materials and processes being used in schools, as well as new hazards which are becoming evident, have made it necessary to issue this new booklet to replace *Safety in practical departments,* No. 3 in the DES Safety Series. This booklet does not attempt to provide a complete guide to safety precautions in all the practical activities that take place in schools (practical activities in science laboratories, for instance, are covered in DES Safety Series No 2[1]), but it will help teachers to be more aware of the kinds of hazards that may exist in their work, and to refer to the expert advice that is available. Practical activities are grouped here under five main subject headings, but other subjects such as business studies have considerable practical elements, and indeed teachers of most subjects of the curriculum will find some of the advice relevant to their work. It will be helpful also to lecturers in further, higher and adult education. The information will be of particular importance to those who are training to teach practical subjects as well as those who are already teaching them. Teachers of subjects involving practical work of the kinds described in this publication are not only concerned with preventing accidents but also with safety education as an essential part of their work. It is important that this introduction should be read in conjunction with each of the chapters that follow. Some items of safety information are of such importance that they are covered in several sections.

Health and Safety at Work etc Act 1974

1.2   The Health and Safety at Work etc Act 1974 applies to schools and its purposes are stated in Section 1 of the Act as:
    'a. securing the health, safety and welfare of persons at work;
    b. protecting persons other than persons at work against risks to health or safety arising out of or in connection with the activities of persons at work;
    c. controlling the keeping and use of explosive or highly flammable or otherwise dangerous substances, and generally preventing the

unlawful acquisition, possession and use of such substances; and

d. controlling the emission into the atmosphere of noxious or offensive substances from premises of any class prescribed for the purposes of this paragraph.'

The Act imposes general duties upon employers, employed persons and others. Sections 15 and 16 of the Act provide for the making of regulations and approved codes of practice in appropriate cases.

1.3   The duties laid upon employers and employees are stated respectively in Sections 2 and 7 of the Act. Teachers and others employed in the education service come within the scope of the Act.

1.4   Pupils are not defined as persons at work but they are directly affected by teaching activities and are covered by Sections 3, 4 and 8 of the Act. Pupils have not been covered by previous health and safety legislation but are now afforded protection for the first time.

1.5   The Health and Safety Executive[2] set up under the Act administers the provisions of the legislation. In educational establishments the responsibility for overseeing the legislation lies with HM Inspectors of Factories, who work in close liaison with HM Inspectors of Schools. Until 1978 HM Inspectors of Factories restricted their visits to educational establishments to the inspection of those parts subject to previous health and safety legislations and to reactive visits, that is to investigate accidents and complaints and to advise when requested. However, Inspectors now have right of entry for the purposes of the Act, and their inspection of educational establishments is likely to form part of the annual inspection programme covering all types of employment.

1.6   Although the scale of work and the use of materials in schools and industry may differ widely, the potential risks are, at times, the same. HM Inspectors of Factories are experienced in widely varying occupational conditions and will apply their expertise in health and safety matters to inspection in schools. In addition to inspection visits Inspectors will give technical advice on safety as the need arises. You can obtain the address of the local inspector from the local authority or from the Health and Safety Executive[2].

1.7   The first objective of inspection will be to ensure that each employing body has an adequate safety policy and has set up the necessary organisation for health and safety within its management structure; that, where appropriate, the precautions that are advised are set out in further detail in departmental or establishment safety policies, arrangements and rules.

1.8   The Health and Safety at Work etc Act provides the opportunity for a new era in occupational health and safety. It is very much a self-regulatory Act which, while recognising the primary responsibility of the employer, places a duty on both the employer and the employed to cooperate in putting and keeping their own house in order as regards health and safety.

1.9   Responsibility for safety information, training and supervision rests with the employing authority. Individual teachers need to appreciate and understand what is safe and what is dangerous in a number of practical activities that range from general matters such as handling, moving and lifting heavy objects to more specialised areas such as the hazards associated with gas, electrical and mechanical appliances which are used in many departments in schools, especially those detailed in this pamphlet. Where initial or subsequent training is considered inadequate, appropriate training is necessary. Courses may be based on nationally agreed formulae (as for first aid) or on modules such as those set out by the Association of Advisers in Craft, Design and Technology[3].

Safety education

1.10   A particularly disturbing feature of industrial accidents is the number which occur to young people under the age of 18, often in the early weeks of their first job. Not only, therefore, must specialist rooms be planned and equipped with safety principles in mind, allowing effective supervision, ease of access to all sections of the working area and sufficient working space for the normal number of pupils, but pupils should be encouraged to develop confidence and a sense of responsibility for themselves and others and to make a just assessment of potential dangers. Every department must have safety rules that are understood and observed. These will vary according to the nature of the premises and equipment and the type of course being offered. Some should appear in written form, but safety cannot be taught through a series of rules alone. Reasons for the rules should be explained, and their wider implications should be discussed from time to time. Pupils should be trained to work sensibly and safely, and to acquire positive attitudes towards the safe practice of a subject. The teacher must give a clear lead by his or her own planning and precepts and by personal example.

Planning of work spaces

1.11   Those who plan and equip rooms for practical work have an important responsibility because it is at the planning stage that basic safety considerations must be examined. Some possible hazards will be obvious, others will be less evident. Where an authority has an inspector or adviser with appropriate responsibility he should be consulted by the architects at the earliest opportunity and be involved in discussions whenever plans have to be changed or modified. Authorities which have no appropriate specialists should ensure that expert guidance is available and that it is properly used.

1.12   Teachers should scrutinise all arrangements within their own rooms to ensure that working conditions are as safe as possible; the positioning of work places and equipment may be crucial in this respect. The safety of working conditions can be impaired by unsuitable heating, ventilation, lighting or floor surfaces, and the influence of wall surface colour on lighting and visibility needs to be considered. Careful attention should always be given to storage of materials, tools, equipment and work in progress. Local education authorities will wish to ensure that appropriate fittings (racks, shelves and cupboards) are installed. Racks should be constructed and supported to resist any tendency to collapse because of uneven loading, or because fixings become loose. Adequate storage space for items such as garments, bags and stools is essential to avoid the danger of clutter. Safety and efficiency can sometimes be achieved by adjusting arrangements for work, for movement and for storage. The resiting of fixed equipment, sanctioned by the appropriate authority, may facilitate easier use and supervision. Floors should not be allowed to become slippery: they should be kept dry and unburnished. The installation of strip lights for general illumination, and of low voltage individual tungsten lamps for certain equipment, are other possible improvements for many practical rooms.

Routine checks

1.13 Accidents occur because of unsafe conditions or unsafe actions. Teachers will wish to institute regular checks on conditions within practical areas. (The checklists for school workshops produced by the Association of Advisers in Craft Design and Technology are particularly useful[3].) The programming of checks is likely to vary according to the frequency with which particular items of equipment are used. Standard routines may also be desirable for the way in which a process or operation is undertaken and for the maintenance of safe conditions within work and storage areas. For example, each pupil may be entrusted with a specific responsibility for allocating and checking tools, perhaps on a rota basis.

Introducing new techniques

1.14 Practical work sometimes involves using a variety of materials, processes and equipment, some of which may not, at first, be entirely familiar to the teacher. While initiative is to be commended, teachers must be alert to possible hazards and ensure that their knowledge is adequate for the detection of dangers, even where these are of a subtle nature, such as the dangers which can arise from enamelling powders. Practical departments in schools have a good safety record but teachers should approach new developments with extra care. Specialised equipment should not be brought into use unless the teacher has acquired the necessary expert knowledge through experience and by attending appropriate courses recognised by the LEA, and is fully conversant with its use and all other relevant considerations (which might include peculiar handling properties, and any special requirements concerning the location and nature of storage). Where a safety hazard is expected to exist, careful thought should be given to the method of teaching and to subsequent work by the pupils. Teachers will wish to exercise careful control of the choice of projects made in school. Some finished objects may prove to be a hazard when used or put to inappropriate use by young people, whilst others require extremely careful and expert supervision while they are being constructed, in order to prevent the possibility of danger to the user. Teachers will also wish to be aware of certain regulations which may affect the making of articles. For example, toys must conform to The Toys (Safety) Regulations 1974 (SI 1367).

Size of groups

1.15   Safety factors need to be taken into account when groups of pupils are allocated to work spaces. In general, rooms are planned for a maximum number according to the area of the room, its shape, and the complexity of the facilities. Other factors may need to be considered. These include the age, ability, experience and aptitudes of the pupils and the nature and range of the work proposed. Care should be taken to ensure that adequate space is available when pupils use tools or operate machines. When activities of a practical nature are organised away from the school premises it is important that sufficient adults are present to give appropriate supervision. Only after careful thought should any pupil be allowed to work alone or out of the sight of a teacher.

Work away from school

1.16   Work outside normal school hours and visits and activities away from school can be a valuable part of education, but possible hazards need to be carefully considered. Teachers will wish to make sure that they are fully aware of the potential hazards in any activity proposed for pupils, and to take adequate precautions to ensure their safety. Work experience, work simulations, community service and conservation activities may require special arrangements to ensure the safety of participants and to give protection to others. A designer, maker or provider of materials, or components has a responsibility to ensure, as far as possible, that recipients and users will be aware of any possible hazards. As is explained in the DES Safety Series No 6[4], the teacher is *in loco parentis;* he or she must take all reasonable care and brief the pupils accordingly. Local education authority regulations must be closely followed; these will sometimes require insurance cover. Pupils engaged in work experience schemes are bound by the legislation applicable to employees of a similar age[5].

Protective clothing

1.17   Unsuitable dress, including certain types of footwear, long hair which is not secured and the wearing of jewellery, may be dangerous. The clothing recommended for use by pupils should be appropriate to the activities so that habits of wearing protective dress are established during school days. Good habits in these respects may assist in a reduction of industrial and domestic accidents. In the event of an accident it may be helpful if pupils' names are clearly visible on their protective clothing. Where there is a risk of dust, sparks, chemical splashes or flying particles affecting the eyes, goggles or industrial spectacles must be worn. Optical spectacles alone do not give adequate protection, and indeed unless they are shatter-proof they present additional hazards. Visors or special goggles to fit over spectacles are necessary. The British Standard on eye protectors gives comprehensive guidance[6]. Protective screens which offer eye protection are also sometimes necessary on a machine. Frequent attention is needed to ensure that such protective devices do not impede vision, and they must be renewed immediately recleaning becomes ineffective. Masks or respirators must be worn in certain conditions; for instance whenever non-soluble or toxic dusts and fumes may arise, when pupils are abrading or machining plastic materials including expanded polystyrene, or working continuously on a polishing machine, or spraying paint and chemicals. Non-disposable masks must be disinfected before and after use, and the filters renewed.

Organisation and other considerations

1.18   One of the aims in teaching practical subjects at all levels should be to develop well organised systematic procedures that contribute both to efficiency and safety. Clutter must be avoided at all times and floor areas must be kept free of garments, bags, materials and rubbish. Storage facilities should be properly used so that their contents are safely located and easily accessible. For example, filing cabinets should be loaded so that they do not topple forward when top drawers are pulled out, the storing of heavy articles should be at low level and materials should never protrude from equipment without adequate marking. Particular care should be exercised when lengthy items, hot materials or sharp edged tools are moved.

1.19   Pupils should not be requested to carry or move heavy articles which could cause physical strain or injury. The need to move equipment frequently is likely to arise in a number of subjects, especially business studies (duplicators, photocopiers and large typewriters), music (hi-fi equipment and heavy musical instruments), and textile work (sewing machines). Any dual purpose equipment must be used with extra care. Drawing desks which are convertible to worktop tables, for example, must be firmly locked in position to prevent sudden movement and the trapping of fingers, or other hazards. Dust and noise should be kept to a minimum, and tools and equipment should be kept clean and tidy. Facilities for washing, for cleaning and for the disposal of waste materials should be kept tidy and well maintained. The disposal of certain waste is controlled by regulations, details of which should be obtained from the local authority. On no account must flammable material be allowed to enter drains.

Fire precautions

1.20 Pupils should be thoroughly familiar with the fire drill and understand the use of fire extinguishers, fire blankets and sand pails. These appliances should be kept inside the workroom as near to the door as possible but remote from that area of the room where the risk of fire is greatest. Rags, cotton waste, polyurethane foam and similar materials are a potential danger and should not be allowed to accumulate or to be stored near naked flames. Aerosol containers should not be stored or used near naked flames or very hot objects, nor should they be punctured even when empty. The local authorities' special requirements must be followed for the storage of flammable materials including some adhesives, many solvents, finishes and other fluids, and for cylinder gases. Storage arrangements for bulk stock differ from those necessary for smaller quantities in daily use. (See Appendices 1, 2 and 3.)

Chemicals

1.21 All corrosive and poisonous chemicals, including many cleaning fluids, adhesives, dyes and inks, must be kept in secure stores under lock and key; quantities in use should be restricted to the minimum necessary. Teachers should be aware of the dangers, including those arising from accidental or intentional inhaling ('glue sniffing'). Procedures for disposal and for action in the event of an accident must be clearly set out in areas where chemicals are stored or used.

Maintenance

1.22 A regular and systematic maintenance scheme for fabric, furniture, fittings, machinery, tools and materials is essential. Maintenance requirements may be increased when practical areas are used by a number of different teachers; where the use extends to further education or to the community generally, responsibilities must be clearly defined. The frequency of maintenance must be related to the intensity of the use and to the nature of the work undertaken. Gifts of equipment including, where necessary, its fitting and adaptation to school use must be approved by the local authority. Some tasks such as renewing grinding wheels may be undertaken only by appropriately qualified persons. The Abrasive Wheels Regulations, 1970 (SI 535) must be complied with.

Electricity and gas

1.23 Portable power tools and a wide range of gas, electrical and mechanical appliances are increasingly used in schools. The potential dangers, the special safety requirements and the importance of proper electrical and gas connections must be known and understood. Any equipment which is faulty should be clearly labelled with a suitable warning. Electrical apparatus should be switched off after use and plugs should be withdrawn from sockets. Main switches and valves should be turned off every night to afford protection and to check and maintain their efficient working order. It should be a rule that whenever the electricity or gas supply is cut off, for any reason, all switches controlling any appliances should be put in the off positions. Ideally, all electrical outlets should incorporate warning lights. (See Appendices 1 and 2.) A notice should be displayed giving information on first aid treatment for electric shock.

1.24   An increasing number of otherwise handicapped pupils and adults are now helped to lead normal lives because of developments in microelectronics, but internal and external pacemakers and other artificial organs may suffer interference from some domestic and workshop electrical equipment which can bruise tissue without damaging the devices them-selves (see Chapter 3 of DES Safety Series No 6[4]). When items of equipment are considered for purchase they should be assessed for interference with known types of artificial organs and rejected if necessary. Suitable notices should be exhibited and unauthorised equipment should be excluded from the work space.

First aid

1.25   Every workroom must have its own first aid box. This should be easily accessible and both teachers and pupils should know where it is kept. The contents should be regularly checked, at least weekly, and the necessary stocks maintained. Teachers should have sufficient knowledge of first aid to offer assistance in the case of accidents which are likely to arise. Pupils should know which member of staff in the school has particular responsibility for the treatment of injuries. The name of this person should be displayed on each first aid box, together with instructions for dealing with burns and electrical shock, the location of telephones and the numbers to ring in an emergency. (See Appendix 4.)

Primary and middle schools

1.26   Much of the content of this pamphlet applies equally to practical work with children below secondary school age. However, specialist accommodation and staffing in many primary and middle schools are often considerably limited, and special consideration needs to be given to safety matters. When practical activities take place within non-specialist areas, equipment may be accessible in situations where it is difficult to arrange the kind of supervision which is normally found in purpose built specialist subject rooms in secondary schools. This could expose the pupils to greater risks, and it is therefore most important that the utmost care is taken to observe proper safety precautions. Safe practice should be an inherent part of the teaching of practical work under any circumstances, and expert advice should be sought whenever the teacher feels that his or her competence to teach a particular aspect of the work falls short of that of the expert.

1.27   Care should be taken to see that areas used for clean and dirty work are separated. Where food is used, a high standard of hygiene should be observed. Food should be stored in a cool clean place away from other materials and equipment.

1.28   Caution should be exercised when requests are received to borrow tools for use by pupils in connection with projects away from the area where craft is normally taught. Generally these should be restricted to tools without a sharp edge; appropriate sets might be housed in trays ready for loan. If the use of sharp edge tools is necessary, care should be taken to ensure that they are used under supervision and that the material being cut is held securely by suitable holding devices. Pupils should be thoroughly trained in the correct methods of carrying tools and other equipment such as wood chisels, hot baking trays and hot irons before they are allowed to walk about with them.

1.29   Extra care is required where any specialist equipment is provided, and non-specialist staff should ensure that they have taken appropriate in-service courses before allowing children to use any of it. The following are examples of such specialist equipment:

- Wood-turning lathes
- Metal-turning lathes
- Mechanical saws (generally for use by teachers and technicians only)
- Brazing equipment (welding equipment is not suitable for use in primary and middle schools).
- Grinding and polishing machines
- Cutting and drilling tools, particularly wood chisels which require special care in their use and maintenance

- Convertible wood/metal benches with heavy fold-back top sections which present a hazard to fingers
- Sewing machines, particularly electric
- Guillotines
- Cooking stoves
- Hand-held electric mixers
- Kilns

1.30 Technicians and other ancillary staff may also require special training for work in primary and middle schools. It is important that their example in the use of tools and equipment is of the highest order. Equipment provided for the use of teachers or technicians, such as circular saws, should be sited in a place not open to the children, or if this is not possible, it should be used only when the area is free from children. The circular saw should be suitably housed or enclosed, and locked at all times when not in use.

1.31 In purchasing electrically powered equipment, including hand mixers, British Standard recommendations[7] and the appropriate sections in this publication should be used as guidelines. Equipment designed for the amateur handyman is often unsuitable for schools. The siting of machines, socket outlets and emergency switches requires expert planning. Electric cables from equipment are likely to cause a hazard if they are allowed to trail across the floor. Electric switches should not be sited near the water supply. An operator should be able to reach and use the controls of a machine without difficulty or risk of obstruction.

1.32 The hazards that arise from working with plastics and the methods of avoiding the dangers associated with certain materials and processes are explained in detail in Appendix 5; these should be carefully studied. The serious dangers of fire, the harmful effects on the skin, the eyes and the lungs that may arise in the manipulation and storage of plastics cannot be emphasised too strongly. Teachers should ensure that the conditions required to avoid the associated hazards are established before work of this kind is undertaken.

Professional advice

1.33   It is again emphasised that this pamphlet is not a comprehensive guide to safe practice and precautions in all the practical activities that take place in schools. Its aim is to indicate the kinds of hazards that are likely to arise, and to draw attention to specific directions and expert advice that are available from many sources including local education authorities, manufacturers, and various organisations, to which teachers should refer for guidance on particular aspects of practical work.

References

1. Department of Education and Science. DES Safety Series No. 2 *Safety in science laboratories.* 1978. HMSO.

2. Health and Safety Executive, 1–13 Chepstow Place, Westbourne Grove, London W2 4TF.

3. Association of Advisers in Craft, Design and Technology, Secretary, Mr F W Elford, London Borough of Hounslow, Civic Centre, Lampton Road, Hounslow TW3 4DN.
The Association has prepared three sets of course elements on safety in the use of heat processes, woodworking machinery and metalworking machinery to enable courses to be arranged that will provide a national minimum standard of safety training for the protection of teachers using school workshop equipment and machinery. It also produces Safe Condition Survey and Report Forms for recording and reporting inspections of school workshops in respect of heat processes, woodworking machinery and metalworking machinery.

4. Department of Education and Science. DES Safety Series No. 6 *Safety at school: general advice.* 1979. HMSO.

5. Department of Education and Science. Circular 7/74. *Work experience.* DES, Stationery Unit, Government Buildings, Honeypot Lane, Stanmore, Middlesex HA7 1AZ.

6. BS 2092 *Industrial eye-protectors.* British Standards Institute, Sales Department, 101 Pentonville Road, London N1 9ND.
The British Standards Yearbook lists current standards and its index should be consulted when a particular item is under consideration.

7. BS 4163 *Recommendations for health and safety in workshops of schools and colleges.*

8. BS 3456 *Specification for safety of household electrical appliances*

2 Art

It is important to read Chapter 1 in conjunction with this chapter, because all its requirements in relation to activities in Art departments are relevant, in addition to the following special needs.

2.1   In recent years it has become increasingly common for a large variety of materials and equipment to be used in art departments. Some of the equipment is power operated and the element of danger consequently needs careful consideration. It is not unusual for a number of different activities to be carried on at the same time in one art room, some of which may demand the use of varied materials and equipment. Where such activities play a major part in the work of the art department, it may be necessary to limit the number of pupils using the studio at any one time.

Accommodation and furnishing

2.2   Safe working largely depends on good design and suitable arrangements in working spaces, especially in machine areas. Space should be allowed for effective movement, and adequate supervision and appropriate lighting should be provided. Storage space is essential so that the floors and passage ways of the working areas may be kept clear of unused materials and equipment. Proper installation and positioning of equipment is important; no machine should be installed under windows where sunlight can make flames and cutting surfaces invisible. The art specialist should study the next chapter as well; the detailed advice there on safety in the use of machines, tools and equipment applies also in art departments. Some problems, however, need to be discussed in detail. Care should be taken in layout to avoid dangerous overcrowding of furniture and equipment. Acoustic treatment of walls, ceilings, and, in the appropriate places, floors should be given close consideration. A good spread of light, both natural and artificial, is of prime importance. Craft activities, particularly those requiring sharp tools, will often need supplementary lighting. Adjustable spotlights can often be helpful but care should be taken to avoid glare or excessively sharp contrasts of light and shade.

Protective clothing

2.3   Suitable protective non-flammable clothing for many activities will reduce the risk of personal injury. Loose-hanging neck ties and long hair can be a hazard when working near machinery. The protection of eyes must receive high priority in every department. Goggles must be used when there is a risk to the eyes, and suitable respirators should be used when dusty materials are being handled. The use of an apron or overall to protect pupils' clothing from paint, dye, plaster and adhesive or clays is clearly a sensible and hygienic practice.

Cutting tools

2.4   Sharp knives and tools are needed for a variety of art work. For the carving of wood or other resistant materials it is important that effective holding devices are employed. For the cutting or engraving of wood, lino or hardboard for printmaking, the use of bench keys, or G-clamps for large blocks, will provide a more stable working surface. Guillotines should be properly guarded at all times.

Electrical equipment

2.5   Advice concerning wiring, proper earthing, correct fuses and systematic inspection is set out in Appendix 1. However, it must be stressed that a number of cut-out switches controlling all power outlets should be placed in readily accessible positions, and an isolator switch of the non self-resetting type should be fitted to each fixed machine. The conversion of hand operated machines to power operation, eg printing presses, should never be undertaken without appropriate professional advice being sought beforehand, and without having the modifications checked by a suitably qualified person before they are used.

Pottery

Kilns   2.6   Kiln doors should be fitted with an approved system to ensure that the mains supply of electricity is turned off before the door can be opened. This may be either a fail-safe positively operated switch (used on some small kilns) or an interlock system, trapped key or similar device. Bright warning lights to indicate that the mains supply is on should be mounted in duplicate in a prominent part of the main studio. Students should have the opportunity to operate kilns, heat treatment being an essential part of the experience in ceramics, but all kilns should be made safe so they can be used by pupils under supervision. Students should be instructed in the complete firing sequence and alerted to the hazards associated with improper removal of ventilation/inspection bungs during firing: blue or 'smoked' glass should always be used to protect the eyes from damage when inspecting temperature colour and flame action. The siting of kilns needs careful attention and adequate space should be allowed around and above them. Extractive ventilation applied by means of a suitable hood and fan system is desirable for any electric kiln that might give off fumes in a working area. Kilns situated in working areas should be caged. The Institute of Ceramics has published detailed advice[1].

Gas kilns   2.7   Gas kilns should not be used in schools unless the staff has had specialist training in firing procedures. All members of staff firing gas kilns should be aware of the 'lockout' procedure and of how to prevent the risk of explosion by blow-back during lighting. A canopy to direct heat and fumes away from the kiln directly to the outside atmosphere is necessary.

Outdoor kilns   2.8   Outdoor kilns should be adequately guarded and fuel should be stored away from heat sources. Care should be taken that smoke and fumes are not blown into surrounding buildings.

Spray equipment   2.9   Spray equipment for the application of glazes should be provided with properly designed extraction booths that are connected to the outside atmosphere. Glazing spray booths that have no outside access for extraction should not be used. All spraying equipment and booths must be regularly washed.

Pug mills   2.10   Pug mills should be operated only by members of staff, and all mills must have securely fixed guards across the loading mouth. All mills should have cut-out switches situated within reach of the operator.

Materials   2.11   The prohibition of raw lead glazes and the precautions in connection with the use of low solubility glazes are set out in DES Administrative Memorandum 517[2]. Those glazes containing over 5 per cent soluble lead should not be used at all in schools, and strict precautions should be taken with all other glazes. Ground flint should not be used for dusting kiln furniture or making batwash. Wherever possible flint should be kept in either slop or paste form.

Ceramic dust   2.12   Floors, working surfaces, tools and overalls should be kept clean and washed regularly. Consideration should be given to the use of industrial vacuum cleaners fitted with suitable filters. Daily cleaning and weekly washing down of all surfaces is necessary on the completion of work in a pottery area. Staff and pupils should wash their hands and dry them, using disposable paper towels. No food or drink should be taken into the studio and it must be stressed that smoking in a studio is extremely dangerous. The use of asbestos material for gloves, batts or shelving in the studio is inadvisable.

Welding

2.13   Attention is drawn to paragraphs 3.32 to 3.39 dealing with gas welding, brazing and electric arc welding. There are a number of dangers to be avoided. Where this work is contemplated, the equipment should be installed only after full advice has been taken from the fire prevention officer and when the teacher is thoroughly competent in its use. If there is no such person on the staff, such equipment should be withdrawn. Nothing less than the completion of a formal course of training in welding should be acceptable as evidence of competence.

Printed textiles

2.14   Wax can be used for various processes in the studio but could become a serious fire hazard, especially if it is heated in a single container over open flames. If hot wax is needed, it should be heated slowly in a specially designed pan suspended in a larger one partially filled with water. Care should be taken to avoid the danger of admission of water to the wax container.

2.15   Some dyes are water or oil emulsions and have to be fixed by placing the fabric in a warm oven. Unless the fabric is thoroughly dry, vapour from these dyes can ignite. Care should be taken to ensure that the storage of such dyes is in a cool place. The preparation of some dyes involves the use of acids and solvents. Acid should always be added to water, never water to acid, as this may lead to a violent reaction. The use of concentrated acetic acid can be avoided by using vinegar instead. Solvents such as methylated spirits carry a fire risk and can also be dangerous, especially to the eyes and if swallowed. Spirits should be stored in a well ventilated metal or stout wooden cupboard away from heat. The cupboard should have a safety base so that if a can were to leak the spirit would be contained. Other dyes requiring boiling water can be hazardous because of the risk of scalding —these dyes should be used only in suitable working conditions.

Photography

2.16   Developers employed in the processing of colour photographic materials, and to a lesser extent those used in processing black and white emulsions may cause an allergic reaction when brought into contact, or prolonged contact, with the skin. Warnings to this effect, together with recommendations for the avoidance of dermatitis, are contained in the printed instructions for the use of chemicals. The processing room should be provided with a 'wet area' for all dish and tank processes and a separate 'dry bench' for printing, enlarging and handling of dry photosensitive materials. Thermometers must not be used as stirring rods and care must be taken to ensure thorough retrieval of any spilt mercury[3].

2.17   The 'wet processing area' should be constructed of chemical-proof material and be provided with a means of washing down all chemically contaminated surfaces after use. Hand rinsing and drying facilities should be provided. Electrical fittings and sockets should be sited away from the 'wet area' and all electrical apparatus should be properly earthed. Generally, it is preferable to fit pull cord type switches in dark rooms.

Other materials and processes

2.18   There is a considerable variety of activities in art departments. When new materials and processes are to be introduced, teachers are urged to consider the possible dangers before activities begin. Written advice from manufacturers or suppliers may be helpful. For example, some varieties of expanded polystyrene give off poisonous fumes when heated to melting point; airborne particles of glass fibre can cause lung damage; resins can cause skin damage; the melting of wax crayons by a naked flame presents a dangerous fire risk. Further advice should be studied in DES Safety Series No 2[4].

Paints   2.19   The danger of paints, crayons and other materials containing poisonous substances is dealt with in DES Administrative Memorandum 2/65[5]. Particular attention is drawn to Appendix 1 of this Memorandum, which lists details of materials commonly used in departments.

Plastics   2.20   Plastics for the most part are safe if used as directed and under appropriate working conditions. It needs to be recognised that some plastic materials are highly flammable; some also give off poisonous vapours. Other types of plastics give off highly toxic vapours when chemicals are in use. The rule to apply in all cases is: when in doubt about materials, consult the manufacturer or consult an authoritative body such as the Plastics and Rubber Institute[6]. When machining plastic materials, masks should be worn. Goggles with shields are recommended when mixing materials. (See Appendix 5.)

Storage   2.21   All materials used in workshops and studios should be kept in suitable unbreakable containers that are clearly labelled. No materials should be mixed in any vessel that might be used for food or drink. Liquids must not be stored in bottles or containers that have been used for food or drink.

Corrosive chemicals   2.22   The preparation, storage and use of corrosive chemicals (particularly acids used in etching processes) need special care and reference should be made to paragraphs 26 and 27 in DES Safety Series No 2[4].

Adhesives   2.23   Adhesives made of cyanoacrylate which are now widely available should not be used by pupils in schools. They have rapid setting qualities and can cause serious problems if they come in contact with the skin; they can stick human skin together within seconds. In certain circumstances, items which have been glued and are apparently secure can disintegrate without warning.

General maintenance

2.24   A list of routine checks relating to the special needs of each department should be included in the school or local authority programme of general maintenance. This list should include all the points raised in this chapter, and a record should be kept either in a log book or an equipment record book. The maintenance calls for a range of technical skills and in some cases a special course of training. Authorities should make sure that competent persons are assigned to this task. The interval between tests should never be longer than a year; when the equipment is in frequent use the interval should be shorter.

Working with glass

2.25   Batch mixing and loading present particular hazards as both silicaceous and toxic dusts are likely to be created. Therefore:
- Adequate extraction and filtering facilities are essential.
- Suitable protective clothing and masks should always be worn.
- If batch material is bought in from a glass-works or supplier the teacher must make sure of its composition.
- Batch should always be mixed in a sealed container, using a properly designed batch house wherever possible.
- The floor and walls of the batch house should be washed regularly.
- Hands should always be thoroughly washed after mixing and loading batch.

2.26   The following points should be noted when hot work is contemplated:
- Suitable eye protection must be worn for furnace work; spectacle glasses should be tempered.
- Clothing made of synthetic materials is not recommended for furnace work; arms should be protected with woollen sleeves; hands should not be covered; suitable footwear must be worn.
- An iron with hot glass just gathered from the furnace, or with cooled

glass, should never be swung.
- Safety spectacles should be worn when removing glass from irons.
- Fuming and lustrous processes should be carried out only in a suitable extraction chamber.
- A kiln used for slumping glass needs precautions similar to those applicable to a kiln for firing ceramics.

2.27   When cutting, grinding and polishing:
- Electrical switches and motors should be well protected from the water used in wet processes; a sensitive earth linkage current breaker unit is a useful safety precaution (See Appendix 1).
- Protective glasses and eye shields should always be worn.
- Loose clothing, ties or sloppy sleeves should not be worn; long hair should be securely fastened back.
- It is essential to ensure that grinding wheels are true and are run at manufacturer's recommended periphery wheel speeds, and that the wheels have no cracks. Worn wheels should not be used (See paragraph 3.43).
- Enough water must always be used on wheels to serve as a coolant as well as to keep down and to remove waste. If this is not done, the glass will tend to fire and could shatter.

2.28   Acid etching and polishing with hydrofluoric acid is a particularly hazardous operation and should be carried out only in further and higher education establishments which are fitted with appropriate fume cabinets, extraction systems and equipment. Work should be carried out only under strict supervision. As soon as facilities for using hydrofluoric acid have been introduced, the nearest casualty hospital must be informed in order that they can keep a stock of internal neutralising agent. The safety procedures to be followed in the event of an accident and the address and telephone number of the casualty hospital must be prominently displayed. Suitable goggles and heavy duty rubber gloves should be worn—gloves should be tested for leaks. It is advisable to wear a further thin pair of rubber gloves underneath the heavy duty gloves, or to powder the hands with a liberal application of whiting. A rubber apron should be worn extending below the tops of a pair of rubber wellington boots, so that any acid splash will not run into the boots. A large plastic dustbin should be kept alongside the work bench full of sodium/bicarbonate/water solution. In the case of an accident the part of the body affected should be immersed immediately. The display of the Health and Safety Executive poster on the dangers of hydrochloric acid is recommended as it offers useful guidance[7].

Conclusion

2.29   The potential dangers inherent in the work of an enterprising art department need not inhibit the initiative of the teachers concerned. It is essential, however, that they be made aware of the risks involved. They should ensure the safety of their pupils as far as possible through careful organisation, good classroom management and close attention to the correct use of materials and equipment. Their personal example will be of great importance.

Art department checklist

How safe is your art room?

1. Do you have a first aid box and accident book in each studio?
    Pupils know what to do in case of an accident.

Glazes

2. Have members of the department recently read the DES Administrative Memorandum 517/55 on lead glazes?

3. Are all manufacturers' instructions strictly adhered to at all times?
    Manufacturers' glazes can be unbalanced by the addition of oxides.

4. Do you know that glaze sprays must not be used and that pottery materials should not be ground unless the studio has a ventilated booth?

5. Do you insist that no food (sweets or drink) is brought into the pottery studio?

6. Do the pupils wash their hands and clean their nails after glazing?
    Glaze fettling must always be done with a knife or sponge rather than finger nails.

Dust

7. Are you aware that the dusting of kiln shelves with flint is hazardous?
    Flint, if required for other purposes, should always be stored in paste or slop form.

8. Do you know that some clay bodies have over 30 per cent free silica?
    Great efforts should be made to keep dust to a minimum. Clay scraps should be cleared and the floor and working surfaces kept clear.

9. Do you know that vacuum cleaners, if used in a pottery studio, are a hazard unless equipped with an industrial filter?

10. If you have blown air central heating is it filtered?
    Filters must be regularly cleaned.

11. How often are class overalls laundered?
    They should be washed weekly.
    All equipment such as sponges, cloths, table tops, should be washed as soon as practicable after use. It is preferable to wash equipment that is already damp rather than to allow it to dry out and present a dust hazard.
    Floors should be wet-swept daily and studios washed down every term.

12. Do you know that asbestos in the form of batts and shelves should not be used in pottery studios?

Electrical hazards

13. Are you satisfied with the electrical safety in your studio?
    Damp concrete floors act as earth connections and are a hazard.

14. Have throwing wheels been checked recently?
    Rubber insulation perishes quickly in damp conditions.

15. Is the power supply to the kilns controlled by a locking switch?

16. Have the kilns any exposed wiring or faulty elements?

17. Do you know that the tying off of element 'fish tails' can be dangerous, and any repairs or modifications to kilns should be carried out only by firms approved by the local education authority?

18. Are all your portable power tools low voltage or double-insulated, and approved by the local education authority?

General precautions

19. Do all machines, eg guillotines, presses and pug mills have adequate guards?

20. Do you remember to use double saucepans when heating wax and doing batik?

21. Is your apparatus for light and colour exercises safe? Has it been checked by an approved electrician?

22. Is the supply of acid for etching or photography carefully controlled?

23. Do pupils know the procedure in the case of an accident?

24. Is your studio equipped with appropriate fire extinguishers in case of emergencies? Do you have a fire bucket and fire blanket?

25. Are all bottles, jars, buckets etc clearly labelled?

26. Do you know that work with plastics, as with aerosols, should not be done unless there is adequate ventilation in the room?
Inhalation of toxic gases may have a delayed reaction—so no danger is immediately apparent.

27. Do you know that the cutting of styrene with a red hot wire can, in badly ventilated conditions, produce fumes that irritate the eyes and cause giddiness?
Children are more prone to this hazard than adults.

28. Do you know that it is safer to use batteries rather than low tension supply fed from the mains for hot wire cutters?

29. Do your pupils wear goggles when using organic liquids, catalysts or machinery?

Plastics

30. Do you know the dangers of directly mixing catalysts and accelerator

31. Do you know that foam materials, unless treated, are highly flammable?
Foam materials must be stored away from heat sources.

32. Do your pupils know what to do when a dangerous substance has come into contact with the eyes?
Immediately bathe with plain water or 2 per cent aqueous solution of sodium bicarbonate; always consult a doctor without delay.

The increasing complexity of equipment and the growing range of materials have added to the danger of accidents in the studio. Young people should be trained to develop a sense of responsibility for their own safety and that of others as part of every day education.

References

1. *Health and safety in ceramics.* Institute of Ceramics, Federation House, Station Road, Stoke-on-Trent ST4 2RY.

2. Department of Education and Science. Administrative Memorandum 517/55 *Restrictions on the use of certain types of glazes in the teaching of pottery.* DES, Stationery Unit, Government Buildings, Honeypot Lane, Stanmore, Middlesex HA7 1AZ.

3. *Mercury—how to handle it and clear up spillage* (L144A) CLEAPSE Development Group,Brunel University, Uxbridge, Middlesex UB8 3PH.

4. Department of Education and Science. DES Safety Series No. 2 *Safety in science laboratories.* 1978. HMSO.

5. Department of Education and Science. Administrative Memorandum 2/65 *Poisonous substances in pencils and other allied materials used in schools.* DES.

6. Education Service of the Plastics and Rubber Institute, Department of Creative Design, Loughborough University of Technology, Loughborough, Leicestershire, LE11 3TU. Tel: Loughborough 32065.

7. Poster: *Danger from hydrofluoric acid* (F2250) Health and Safety Executive, 1–13 Chepstow Place, Westbourne Grove, London W2 4TF.

3 Craft, design and technology

It is important to read Chapter 1 before and in conjunction with this chapter because all its requirements in relation to workshops and workshop activities are relevant, in addition to the following special needs. Additionally, recommendations relating to the design of equipment, machinery, tools and work places will be found in BS 4163[1], a copy of which should be available in all schools with workshop facilities.

The planning of workshop areas

3.1 The principles governing the design of new workshops were dealt with in Building Bulletin 31[2]. The safe use of rooms used for the teaching of craft, design, and technology (CDT) is largely dependent on the layout of equipment, flooring, lighting, heating and colour schemes. Teachers, in conjunction with their advisers, should look critically at their existing workshop arrangements to ensure that the working conditions are as safe as possible. The rearrangement of the benches may increase the width of the gangways, and the re-siting of fixed equipment, with the approval of the head teacher and the local education authority, may well permit easier supervision of the room. The installation of strip fluorescent lighting for general illumination, and of low voltage individual lights for certain equipment, is another possible improvement. The wiring regulations of the Institution of Electrical Engineers[3] should be observed. See also the advice in Appendix 1.

3.2 Workshops should be warm. If hands are cold they are less sensitive, and if machines or hand tools are very cold they can be handled only with a much reduced degree of safety. Some floor surfaces may become burnished by sawdust and shavings, causing slippery conditions. Cleaning methods should guard against this possibility; special adhesive pads, set flush with the floor, give very good protection, as do some other non-slip treatments. A well organised, attractive workshop, where the British Standard colour coding[4] is used to identify and to provide a warning against danger, and where appropriate precautionary notices are properly displayed, is a lesson in itself.

3.3 Careful attention should always be given to the storage of materials and partly finished work. Local education authorities should ensure that appropriate fittings (racks, shelves and cupboards) are installed. Racks should be constructed and supported to resist any tendency to collapse because of uneven loading, or because fixings become loose. Great care should be exercised on the storage of lengths of timber and heavy section metal, especially when these are vertically racked. Care should also be taken when lengths of timber and metal are stacked horizontally, as projecting sawn ends could cause painful and serious injury to both teachers and pupils. Special storage arrangements are needed for certain combustible materials such as resins. Clutter is a source of danger, so there is a need for adequate storage for garments, bags, stools etc.

3.4   Workshops should be considered as places with definite zones of work. If suitable arrangements are made for storing the relevant equipment and tools in each zone unnecessary movement can be reduced considerably, and the workshop will become more efficient—and thus a safer place for the pupils. Suites of workshops are often planned for new schools with machine bays, hot-working areas and constructional spaces leading to outside covered aprons. In these cases it is important for the teacher to be able to exercise supervision of the pupils from the main workshop, if necessary through suitably glazed screens.

Precautions

3.5   Potential sources of danger are listed overleaf. Special vigilance is necessary in any situations that give rise to potential dangers under these headings.

Personal care and protective equipment

3.6   It is especially important that pupils should regard the protection of eyes, skin and clothing in particular as part of the normal procedure essential to the performance of any operation where danger is likely to arise. The teacher's example in this matter is of paramount importance. The protection of eyes must receive high priority in every school workshop. The cutting tools of certain machines need to be suitably guarded; these precautions are mentioned in a later section which deals with metalworking machines. In any work which may give rise to danger to the eyes, for example from flying particles, appropriate eye protection should be provided according to the degree of risk. Any person actually engaged in such activity will require eye protection as specified in BS 2092[6]. Some timbers and plastic materials produce highly irritant dust when being sanded: a face mask should be used to protect the lungs, mouth and nose. Helmets with visors, leather aprons, gloves, gaiters or spats, together with

Potential sources of danger

Insecurity
: bodily balance, lifting and carrying, location of work and equipment, tool handles.

Sharp edges
: including all cutting tools and saws.

Closing movements
: where flesh and clothing may be nipped.

Rotating parts
: of all descriptions, particularly where they produce an ingathering nip or intake.

Reciprocating parts
: such as rams running close to fixed objects and forming trapping points.

Emissions
: including heat, sparks, fumes and dust.

Fire
: from foundry work, forging, brazing torches, burners and soldering irons.

Electrical faults
: especially in circuits used for machinery and equipment.

Flash and glare
: from welding and other equipment.

Explosions
: disintegrations such as molten metal on damp surfaces, or abrasive wheels badly mounted.

Noise
: which can be harmful in itself, but can also conceal signals which will alert a teacher to potential dangers[5].

Clothing
: which can be unsuitable and provide inadequate protection.

Note. The fly press is an example of a machine which needs siting, guarding and supervision to avoid some of these potential sources of danger; it should be locked when not in use.

substantial footwear are essential when pupils assist in the pouring of molten metals into a mould. The mould must be carefully positioned and stable. The special protection needed for pupils who are welding is dealt with in paragraphs 3.32 to 3.39 below.

3.7   The importance of bodily protection must be stressed by imposing an obligation to wear aprons, overalls or similar garments. Where necessary these should be made of flameproof and chemically resistant material. Periodic inspection is necessary to ensure good maintenance of these garments, because ingrained dirt and oil, loose clothing, unfixed belts and apron strings are a serious source of danger. The pupils should remove their jackets, roll up their shirt sleeves and secure their ties. It is very important that they should wear substantial footwear, with any laces properly secured. Leather or other thick aprons are necessary for pupils working at the forge as a protection against hot scale and sparks. No pupil with long, uncontrollable hair should be allowed to operate any machine. Standard requirements should establish habits of wearing the right clothing for the job.

3.8   Handling certain materials, including mineral oils, can be harmful. Barrier cleansing creams should be used. It should be the custom for pupils to wash their hands before going to the toilet as well as afterwards. Disposable gloves, as well as barrier creams, are necessary when using many synthetic materials and adhesives. A cleansing cream should be used immediately on completion of the process, and the hands should be washed straightaway. Any recommended antidotes or special solvents must always be kept available. The range of cyanoacrylate adhesives should not be used by pupils in schools. Toxic hazards are usually caused by the evaporation of solvents: it is desirable that such fumes should not enter the workshop, but if this is unavoidable, adequate ventilation must be arranged. The risk of fire and explosion can be minimised by storing such materials, properly marked, in a cool place; by sensible disposal of waste; by the use of special detergents instead of solvents for cleaning; and by strict adherence to the maker's recommendations and to those of BS 4163[1].

General workshop processes

3.9   The prevention of injury from hand tools depends, in the first instance, on the tools being well maintained. Adequate staff time and/or assistance is needed for this purpose. The pupils must be given careful training in the correct use of the tools and the teacher should maintain an appropriate standard of class discipline in the workshop. The dangers of blunt tools, of deformed clamps and spanners, of loose hammer heads or chipped hammer faces, of files insecure in old handles and of dangerous burrs on tools and work, are well known. The replacement of worn bench stops, sawing boards and vice cheeks and the resurfacing of benches are also important. Well displayed, clearly labelled tool storage facilities are one of the best ways of ensuring that the correct tools are used for particular jobs. Separate tool kits should be made up for outside work.

3.10   The provision of benches of varying heights will help to ensure that pupils use an appropriate one. Duckboards are a source of danger and should not be used. It is easier and safer to work at a bench which is a little too low than at one which is too high.

Power-driven equipment[1]   3.11   When a workshop containing power-driven equipment is not directly under the supervision of the teacher, it is a wise precaution for him to lock the re-set switch controlling the workshop power in the off position.

3.12   Emergency stop switches and all isolator switch systems should be tested regularly to ensure that they work reliably.

3.13   Work on a particular machine which is carefully planned and phased throughout a course will help the pupils to appreciate the importance of the safety procedures. Only one pupil may be allowed to operate a machine at a time; if another pupil is allowed to help or to observe he should stand clear of the controls, in a safe position, and refrain from distracting the operator's attention.

3.14   Pupils should be taught to isolate a machine before any adjustment is made to it. Adjustments and cleaning must be done with the machine at rest. Machines must always be switched off before being left unattended.

3.15   The main causes of the accidents inherent in the use of machine tools are in the nature of the machine itself, in the apparent simplicity of certain operations and in the deceptive appearance of slowly moving parts. In some machines, or machine parts, however, the danger is obvious enough; sharp cutting edges of tools and fast running machinery are but two examples. But danger may not always be so apparent: an accident can be caused through overconfidence or lack of concentration on the part of the user. For this reason it is often a sensible precaution for the teacher to check all work and tools before a machine is switched on. Tools should be sharpened so that swarf is broken into small pieces. Work must be firmly secured. Suitable cutting speeds must be selected and chuck keys, spanners, etc, must be removed before machines are switched on. Pupils should be taught to describe and discuss work without pointing to the parts, and generally only after switching off the machine. Moving parts should never be stopped by hand friction. A notice, fixed on or near a machine, giving instructions about operating methods is likely to be helpful to pupils.

3.16   Good workshop maintenance is essential. Floor areas near machines must be kept clear, clean and well marked. Any spilt oil or water must be mopped up immediately and wood shavings must be removed frequently to prevent burnishing, which makes floors slippery. Machines must be kept clean and clear of swarf; it should be removed by using small handbrushes, not cloths.

Metalworking processes and machines
See also publications by the Association of Advisers in Craft, Design and Technology[7].

Forgework   3.17   It is a wise precaution to limit the number of pupils working at a forge to two in number. The transfer of hot metal from the forge area to other places should not be tolerated[1].

Acids for pickles and micro-etching   3.18   Non-acidic pickling solutions should be used wherever possible. In general baths of acid pickle should be sited close to the water supply and/or a rinsing tank, and below bench level to minimise the risk of eye injuries through accidental splashing of acid. Protective goggles should be worn. No equipment or switches should be located behind the pickling bath area. The bath should be located in a ventilated cupboard or have a lid, either of which can be locked when not in use. Acid solutions for pickling must be made up by the teacher or the technician. The water must always be put into the bath before the acid is carefully added. The use of concentrated acid or a mixture of sulphuric and nitric acids as a mordant for etching increases the potential dangers. Any spillage of acids should be carefully and quickly dealt with by neutralising with sodium carbonate powder before wiping up with a cloth or paper, which should be disposed of in such a way as not to cause further damage.

3.19   Main stocks of acid should be kept in a central store provided with a low sited, ventilated and lockable cupboard, lined with acid resistant material such as ceramic tiles, lead, stainless steel or stone. Only a limited supply of concentrated acid should be kept in the workshop, and this should be in a cupboard which is strong, stable and properly locked. Acid must be kept in standard type acid bottles, and these should be clearly labelled and always carried with both hands. Glass stoppers or plastic caps should be replaced and the bottles returned to store immediately after use[1].

3.20   Provision of facilities for immediate irrigation of the eye or washing of the affected part of the body with water is essential to minimise the danger of acid burns. Clean water from a plastic bottle, delivered as an upward jet, gives effective eye irrigation but acid burns to the eyes should be referred to the local eye clinic for further treatment. (See Appendix 4.)

Finishes   3.21   The regulations made under the Petroleum Acts apply to schools. A separate lockable cupboard or store, made of fire-resistant material is necessary for containing flammable finishes. Depending on the quantities stored, the store should be adequately vented to the outside with the vent openings protected on the inside with a copper gauze of not less than 1mm mesh. If possible the store should be located in a safe place outside the workshop. Although there may be occasions when the use of spray equipment is an advantage, its use with certain finishes inside a building gives rise to fire risk and pollution problems which can be solved satisfactorily only by the construction of a special booth. This provision can only rarely be contemplated in schools and expert advice should always be sought beforehand[1].

3.22   Care should be taken when using solvents for cleaning brushes and removing spillage, because of eye, skin, respiratory and fire hazards. Rags soaked in solvents should be placed in a metal bin out of doors as soon as possible. The use of solvents to cleanse the skin should be avoided as these may be harmful, and the use of proprietary skin cleaners is advisable. Benzene is a chronic poison and should on no account be used in schools for this purpose.

3.23   If electro-plating or anodising is to be attempted, an area of the workshop should be planned for the purpose. Expert advice should always be taken before any but the simplest processes are used, because of the dangers arising from the use of caustic solutions and other toxic substances. This applies to the installation of the equipment, to the storage of chemicals and electrolytes, and to their use in schools[1].

Soft soldering   3.24   A separate bench covered with stainless steel and provided with fixed gas connections and a suitable power point is required. A bunsen burner is occasionally used for soft soldering. The flame may be almost invisible in bright daylight; and screening from windows is desirable. Care should be exercised if corrosive fluxes are used because of the dangers to hands and eyes. Solders containing cadmium should not be used.

Moulding and casting   3.25   A serious accident can be caused by the explosive vaporisation of moisture by molten metal, and under no circumstances should the furnace and casting area be within easy reach of water taps or boshes. A sidescreen may obviate any danger. The floor must be clear of all obstructions[1].

3.26   Clear instructions should be given to the whole class about the procedure to be followed when molten metal is poured and the pouring should take place only under the personal supervision of the teacher. He should also supervise the working and drying of the moulds, the cleaning, coating and pre-heating of any steel tools which may come into contact with the molten metal and the melting of the metal. Special care is needed to ensure that equipment for handling crucibles is efficient. Refractory crucibles need to be inspected frequently; they should be replaced when they become cracked or worn. Pupils involved in the pouring operation need body protection in the form of helmets and visors, leather aprons, gloves and spats or gaiters together with substantial footwear. Teachers and technicians regularly involved in the casting of molten metal should be provided with the full range of protective clothing including boots. Any pupil who may be watching should stand sufficiently far away to escape the risk of being splashed with molten metal. When the two halves of the moulding box are closed they should be carefully weighted or suitably clamped together, to prevent them opening when the metal is poured. A tray set flush with the floor and containing 50mm depth of dry sand provides a suitable refractory surface on which to stand the crucible and moulding box during the pouring operation. The tray should be of adequate size but not so large as to be a hazard. Magnesium alloys are potentially dangerous because they are often highly inflammable. They must not be used in school workshops. For this reason the source and composition of any metal must be tested before use.

Brazing   3.27   The floor surrounding the hearth should be well maintained and free of loose articles and materials. Generally one pupil only should be allowed to work at each hearth at a time. A procedure for checking all hoses and connections at regular intervals should be established. Brazing torches should be extinguished when not in use. Where the gas is from mains supply the whole of the installation in each work area should be controlled by a well positioned emergency master valve. This should be turned off every night to afford protection and to ensure that it is kept in effective working order. A non-return valve is necessary in the gas line of each torch and a solenoid valve may be desirable on the gas supply. Effective extraction should be provided in order to remove any toxic fumes produced during brazing[8].

3.28   When liquefied petroleum gas (LPG) is used, the correct type of torch must be selected, by referring to the manufacturer if necessary. Teachers responsible for using LPG equipment should be familiar with the British Standard[1]. The correct operating pressure of the torch must be checked. If it is designed to operate at a pressure lower than that of the cylinder, a low pressure regulator must be used.

3.29   Only the approved type of hose should be used and care should be taken to ensure that the hose is not damaged, kinked or burnt. The hose should not be coiled around the cylinders while in use. It should be as short as practicable, while allowing adequate separation between the cylinder and the working nozzle. The ends of the hose should always be cut squarely across, and should be securely fixed to unions and torches with approved hose clips. LPG is heavier than air and any leakage will tend to flow to low levels. Mixed with air LPG becomes a flammable explosive mixture and its ignition will result in the flame travelling back along the vapour track to the point of leakage. Checking for leaks should be done with soap or detergent solution, never with a naked flame. If a leak is suspected all flames must be extinguished and the cylinder valve must be turned off. Any leaking cylinder should be labelled clearly and taken outside to a safe place, away from drains and from any source of ignition. Under no circumstances should LPG be used in or over a motor vehicle maintenance pit, as any leakage of the gas will accumulate in the pit and cannot be dispersed.

3.30   For safe operation it is important that the equipment is checked by the teacher before allowing pupils to use the appliance, and that the torch is ignited by a spark igniter immediately the gas is turned on. When the torch is being rested, it should be supported vertically by a conveniently placed cradle, and the flame should be extinguished if it is not needed for a while. When the appliance is closed down the cylinder valve should be turned off and the flame allowed to burn out before the torch controls are closed. It is not necessary to dismantle the appliance from the cylinder for short-term storage but the hose should be carefully coiled, avoiding strain in the connections. When not in use the cylinder should be stored at ground level in an upright position and in a well ventilated area. Any necessary cleaning of the jet should be done with a stiff bristle, and not a wire pricker.

3.31   LPG is not in itself a poisonous gas but adequate ventilation is necessary to prevent carbon monoxide poisoning which can be caused by incomplete combustion, and to prevent an accumulation of gas/air mixture approaching a flammable concentration. If brought into prolonged contact with the skin, the rapid evaporation of the liquid gas may cause severe frost burns, which would require immediate medical attention[1]. (See also Appendix 2.)

Gas welding and cutting   3.32   The introduction of welding techniques will normally be reserved for senior pupils who have satisfactorily completed a metalwork course, which includes hard soldering. The head of the school must understand that there are a number of dangers to be avoided and, where a course is planned, he must satisfy himself that the teacher is thoroughly competent to use the equipment. It is not sufficient, for example, that a teacher has 'picked up' some handiness in the use of welding apparatus; this can be quite inadequate and even dangerous if he is unaware of the precautions that have to be taken. Furthermore, knowledge of what to weld is just as important as knowing how to weld[1]. (See Appendix 2.) The Association of Advisers in Craft, Design and Technology has issued details of minimum standards of safety training[7].

3.33   Provision for gas welding may be made in two ways.
- Cylinders may be mounted on a trolley and used in conjunction with a suitable welding bench. In this case the equipment has to be safeguarded, not only when it is in use, but also when it is not. It may be wheeled to an adequately ventilated and safe place. If the equipment is locked away the door should be boldly marked with the appropriate symbol indicating the location of the cylinders, and arrangements must be made so that it can be quickly removed in case of fire.
- Cylinders may be housed in a ventilated external storage chamber with light fire resistant roof and the gases piped to the welding bench.

Which method should be used, and the design of any fixed installation, are matters for detailed discussion between the architect and other officials —the chief fire prevention officer and the customer installation engineer of the company supplying the gases.

3.34   Whichever method is employed there are standard precautions to be observed in maintaining and operating the oxy-acetylene welding and cutting equipment. It should be used in a suitable, cleared area specially equipped for this purpose, and should be done only on a base made of refractory materials. Adequate ventilation is essential, especially when (on rare occasions in school) galvanised materials are being welded or cut.

3.35   Pupils using welding equipment, as well as close observers, require strict supervision by a competent teacher of welding. The eyes of operators and close observers must be protected from glare and sparks, and they must wear appropriate protective clothing and adequately substantial footwear. Guidance on eye protection and protective clothing is given by the British Standards Institution in BS 1542[8] and BS 2653[9]. When the equipment is assembled tests should be made for leaks with a soap or detergent solution, but never with a naked flame. Cylinders should always be placed away from any source of heat. Precautions should be taken to avoid burning or damaging the hoses. All fittings should be kept free of oil, grease or dirt, and torches should be checked regularly and maintained in good condition.

3.36   Acetylene will burn instantly from a spark or even hot metal, and when present in the air in any quantity is liable to explode. It should never be used in schools at a pressure above 9 psi g. In case of backfire (gas burning inside the torch) or flashback (explosion of gas between regulator and torch) both oxygen and acetylene cylinder valves must be closed immediately[1]. (See also Appendix 2.)

Electric arc welding   3.37   The most frequent problem associated with electric arc welding is the risk of a painful form of flash blindness. The danger is greater with pupils using tools and equipment in the workshop than with the operator who is welding and who is unlikely to be tempted to observe without his protective visor. A booth, shielded by metal screens extending at least from 1 metre to 1.75 metres above the ground, will effectively protect other pupils from direct flash. It is important also to screen any windows through which any direct flash may be harmful to pupils or others passing by. Ventilation must be adequate and the installation of an extractor fan may be necessary. When the welding apparatus is being used, nearby workshop windows should be opened to obtain a through draught. The equipment must have a properly earthed transformer (see Appendix 1) and the teacher should ensure that the return path of the electric current is satisfactory before switching on. A separate lead from the work piece to the mains earth should be fitted as an additional safety measure. Only welding systems with an open circuit voltage of not more than 50 volts should be used in schools. A booklet published by the Health and Safety Executive gives guidance on electric arc welding[10].

3.38   The pupil operating the equipment should wear a leather apron and gloves and must use a welding mask at all times. The helmet type of mask is preferable as it removes any temptation the pupil may have to lower it from his eyes. The electrode holder should have a guard to protect the hand from the arc and from the live portion of the electrode. Useful guidance on arc welding is given in BS 638[11].

3.39   Much of the advice including the previous section on gas welding is applicable to electric arc welding. In particular the use of the equipment must be properly understood by the teacher before instruction is given to pupils[1].

Shearing machines

3.40   When a manually operated sheet-metal shearing machine is not being used it should be made safe by removing the handle, or securing the handle to a suitable fixture, or fitting a stout pin into the hole in the blades. Foot operated machines should be used only by the teacher or technician, and should not be situated in areas to which pupils have free access[1].

Centre lathes

3.41   Most pupils will use the lathe early in the metalwork course. The complexities of the machine can therefore be introduced gradually and this will help to ensure that the pupils understand the importance of safe methods of operating. At all times when they are using a lathe pupils should be protected from injury by a chuck guard. Personal eye protectors should be worn as a protection against eye injury. A suitable transparent screen attached to the machine may be desirable for certain cutting operations. If a school lathe is not equipped with a coolant pump, care should be taken when the coolant is applied with a brush. Accidents can occur when swarf is being removed from turned work, and it is advisable to have a simple hook available for this purpose, which should be used only when the machinery is stationary. Special care should be taken when very heavy attachments are changed on certain lathes, and in many instances the teacher will wish to change them himself. He should check that all attachments are properly secured before a pupil switches the machine on. Hand-held tools need special care. Whenever cloth is used it should be in pieces too small to wrap around turned work when it revolves. If spinning is undertaken, the set-up of the lathe must be inspected by the teacher, and the job must be made safe by 'locking' the disc of metal over the forming chuck. Material which is fed through the hollow mandrel of the headstock should be adequately guarded at the free end, and an excessive length of metal overhanging the lathe should be avoided. If a lathe has a hollow mandrel in which a pupil's finger might be damaged, it is a wise precaution to plug the open end of the mandrel with a rubber bung when it is otherwise exposed. Correct cutting speeds and feeds are essential for safety and efficiency, and teachers should ensure that the principles of these are included in the course, and that pupils understand the methods of obtaining correct speeds and feeds.

3.42   Tools and accessories must be positioned so that the operator does not have to lean over the machine to obtain them. Suitable provision should also be made for drawings and job sheets[1].

Grinding machines   3.43   Pupils should wear safety spectacles when they use any type of grinding machine[1]. Teachers must frequently check that tool rests are close to the grinding wheels. Dual-purpose machines for grinding and polishing are not recommended. Grinding wheels may be fixed and changed only by qualified persons. Teachers should be familiar with the Abrasive Wheels Regulations 1970 (SI 535) and with the advice of the Health and Safety Executive[12].

Polishing machines   3.44   Spindles of buffing machines must be guarded by sleeving and the unprotected end of the spindle covered. Leather gloves may be worn but a cloth or an apron should on no account be used to hold work while it is being buffed—work should be held against the lower portion of the buffing wheel which is revolving away from the operator[1].

Drilling machines   3.45   It is important that the correct drilling speeds are used. A drill chart should be displayed close to the machine. Work should be securely held, either with a machine vice or a clamp. Special care is needed when further support is required for large pieces of work. At least one machine table should be available which is slotted and the accessories should include a range of equipment for clamping the work when necessary. A collar or other device will prevent the table slipping down the pillar. The machine must be switched off when securing or moving the work piece.

3.46   A chuck guard must always be used. The design of the guard should be such that there is easy access to the chuck, that coolant can be satisfactorily applied, that it allows the cutting edge of the drill and the work to be clearly seen, and that vision is not obscured by the action of coolant, oil and swarf. Spindles, whether splined or plain, thrust races and belt and pulley spindle drives should be guarded. Most modern machines are well protected in this respect but some older machines may require modification[1,13].

Shaping machines   3.47   The ram of the machine should be fully guarded. Before the machine is switched on, checks should be made to ensure that the ram driving clamp is securely tightened, the workpiece is securely fixed and clear of the path of the ram, and all operating handles are removed. Hands should be kept clear of the machine, and no attempt should be made to adjust the stroke, the position of the workpiece on the table, or the tool in the holder while the ram is in motion, or before the machine has been electrically isolated[1].

Milling machines   3.48   Great care should be exercised in teaching milling operations. The dangers which are known to arise in the course of ordinary working and from dangerous practices should be discussed. It is of primary importance that milling machine cutters must always be guarded as completely as possible to suit the cutter being used and the operation being carried out, without impairing vision. Particular care should be taken to protect pupils from the underside of the cutter on horizontal machines when the work is traversed to and from the cutter. The following points should be emphasised.

- The workpiece should always be securely fixed in a balanced position on the machine table.
- The cutters must always be turning in the correct direction.
- Safety limit stops must be fixed.
- The machine must be isolated when a cutter or arbor is being changed.
- Milling cutters with multiple sharp edges require careful handling.
- A cutter with a damaged tooth should never be used.
- Mating surfaces should be kept clean to prevent locking of parts, wear and distortion, which cause dangerous situations.
- An arbor support should be used in the most effective position whenever there is danger of distortion to the arbor.
- The table traversing handle must be disengaged before automatic feeds are engaged.
- The soluble oil feed spout must be directed down on to the workpiece before the pump is switched on.
- The machine table must be kept free of tools, and swarf must be cleared frequently with a brush, but only when the machine is stationary[1,14].

Woodworking processes and equipment

Hand tools   3.49   Both the chisel and the saw can be dangerous tools if wrongly or carelessly used. Correct stance and the positioning of the hands must be taught. It is essential that the wood should be held securely.

Wood trimming guillotine and mitre trimmer

3.50   Although hand-operated, this machine is highly dangerous and is not recommended for school use. For the unwary, it can easily result in the amputation of a finger end. If a mitre trimmer is installed in a workshop senior pupils should be allowed to use it only after careful instruction by the teacher. It should be locked when not in use[1].

Woodworking machinery

3.51   Some woodworking machinery, such as circular saws and planing machines, is notoriously dangerous and if it is installed in a school it should be for the use of teachers and technicians only. Properly designed, separate machines should be installed; improvised, dual-purpose or multi-purpose machines, including portable saws and circular saw attachments to wood-turning lathes, generally have no place in a school workshop. Reference should be made to Health and Safety Executive's booklet, *Safety in the use of woodworking machines*[15], and to the advice on use of woodworking machinery from the Association of Advisers in Craft, Design and Technology[7].

3.52   It must be possible for the teacher to lock the isolator switch of the machines in the off position. It cannot be assumed that every teacher of workshop crafts is experienced in the use and maintenance of woodworking machinery and there should, therefore, be a rule that the competence of the teacher to use the machines should be confirmed before he is allowed to use them. Classes which provide expert instruction in these matters are available at most colleges of further education. The teacher should avoid using the specialised woodworking machinery when a class is present and when his attention is easily distracted. Lack of concentration through divided attention might easily result in an accident, either to the teacher himself or to the pupils working in the workshop[1].

Wood-turning lathes

3.53   Wood-turning lathes are best placed where there is good natural lighting and away from parts of the workshop that are in frequent use by the pupils. The end of a long wall away from the workshop entrance and from the storeroom is a suitable position. The lathe is often sited parallel to a wall with the operator facing the wall or the centre of the room. Sometimes the headstock of the lathe is in the corner of the room and the bed at an angle to the wall. If there is room to work round the headstock, this latter position may be the safest.

3.54   Provided that careful instruction is given by a teacher who is himself an experienced wood turner, wood-turning lathes can be used with safety in schools. Slow speeds and scraping tools are advisable for beginners, although speeds may be increased and the use of the gouge can be introduced as the pupil's confidence develops. Timber should always be carefully inspected for defects. The use of jointed or laminated blocks of wood is hazardous, and special precautions are necessary to prevent breakage; even so, lower speeds should be selected. The dual use of one lathe—one pupil turning between centres or on the main face place while another is working on the outside face plate—should be strictly forbidden. The outside face plate carrying a heavy job may become unscrewed if pressure between the cutting tool and the work is not maintained as the lathe is stopped or slowed down. This is particularly important on machines fitted with a brake or with a reversing switch. The utmost care should be taken to ensure that work fixed to a face plate by screws is secure.

3.55   Turning tools should always be maintained in a sharp condition, and should be stored in a small trolley or rack conveniently placed under or alongside the lathe. The rack should not be fixed behind the lathe, nor should tools be placed on the bed of the lathe. A draughtsman's smock is an excellent protective garment for a pupil using the lathe, but if an apron is worn the strings should be tied behind the back. Personal eye protectors should always be worn. During the introductory lessons, the teacher must check the work to be turned for security and clearance, the lathe for correct speed and the tee rest for height, clearance and rigidity. Where a considerable amount of turning is done the dust produced may present a problem. Normally, however, extraction equipment above the lathe is not required. Timbers that produce irritant dust should not be turned.

Circular saws   3.56   The saw itself should be so guarded, equipped and maintained as to conform to the standards of safety prescribed by the Woodworking Machinery Regulations 1974 (SI 903) made under the Factories Act. The guard should always be in the correct position and the underside of the saw table needs to be adequately guarded. It is not always realised that the correct design of the riving knife and its positioning are as important as the correct adjustment and use of the guard. The riving knife must be in position when timber is cut because the wood may trap the back of the saw and rise from the table at a startling speed. The riving knife should be about 10 per cent thicker than the plate of the saw but thinner than the saw kerf. In order that it may act as a guard and splitter, the knife should be aligned with the blade and should always be within 12mm of the saw teeth.

3.57   The saw fence should not be overlong or the wood may pinch on to the saw, thus causing danger. It should guide the wood up to the teeth of the saw but not more than 30 or 40mm beyond. The distance between the saw blade and the delivery end of the saw bench table should not be less than 1200mm.

3.58   Where the spindle of a circular saw may be operated at more than one working speed, no saw blade should be used which has a diameter of less than 60 per cent of the diameter of the largest saw blade which can be properly used at the fastest working speed of the spindle. A notice must be fixed securely to the saw specifying the diameter of the smallest saw blade which may be used in the machine. The saw blade must be properly sharpened and set; inaccuracy or neglect in either respect can cause an accident. Saw blades should be regularly checked for cracks, particularly near the gullet. A cracked saw must not be used. Properly shaped push sticks and push blocks must always be to hand and must be used for any cut within 300mm of the end of the cut or to remove cut pieces of material from between the saw blade and the fence. Unless a saw blade is correctly tensioned, it will not run true and will not cut accurately. If by any means a saw blade becomes overheated, it should be returned to the maker for retensioning[1].

Planers   3.59   When a planing machine is installed, the correct setting of the knives in the cutter block is very important. 1mm is the maximum overhang, and after grinding, the correct balance of the blades should be checked. Timber should not be forced through the machine or planed against the grain; nor should short pieces of timber be planed. A 'bridge' guard complying with the requirements of the Woodworking Machinery Regulations should be provided on every planing machine, and should be used in the correct manner. The part of the cutter block exposed behind the fence should be guarded[1].

Band saws and jig-sawing machines

3.60   If a band saw is included in the woodworking equipment, the blade should be completely guarded except between the table and the top guide. The bottom mouth of the band saw table should be replaced when it becomes worn. If a jig-sawing machine is installed, the belt and pulley should be enclosed[1].

Mortisers

3.61   Only hollow-chisel mortisers are appropriate for school work[1].

Drilling machines

3.62   The advice in 3.45 and 3.46 above applies here too.

Portable electric equipment[1]

3.63   For general information about installation, maintenance and testing of equipment, siting of power sockets, earthing of appliances and safety regulations refer to Appendix 1.

3.64   Increasing use is being made of portable electric tools both in schools and in the home. Before buying any such equipment a school should seek approval from the local education authority, which will have an agreed policy about its use. In reaching a decision the authority will have in mind the possible dangers arising from faulty earth connections, especially if the equipment may be used near water pipes, other earth connected equipment, on concrete or damp floors. Such dangers may be reduced by using only equipment of a lower voltage (usually 110 volts) or by specifying only machines which meet the stringent 'double-insulation' requirements of the British Standards Institution[16].

3.65   Portable machines should be robust; attachments which extend the machine beyond its normal use should not in general be used. Adequate plugs, sockets and cables should be fitted and standard colour coding should be observed. A system for regular checking by the teacher and for periodic expert examination should also be established. Particular attention should be given to leads and extensions in respect of their capacities, the avoidance of overloading when wound around a reel, and the need to prevent dangers of tripping over trailing cables[1].

Outside activities

3.66 Some activities may take place on outside sites, such as those undertaken for community service or with other agencies. The general principles already described apply to all practical work with tools, materials and components wherever it takes place. When work outside the workshop is undertaken teachers should ensure that the pupils are ready for this added responsibility, that they have received adequate instruction in the use of the necessary tools, and that no person ever works alone.

3.67 Where larger constructions of a permanent or semi-permanent nature are considered, detailed plans must be agreed with the appropriate departments of the local authority. Care should be exercised by the teacher to ensure that no pupil is subjected to additional dangers, for instance, through working at a height or lifting heavy weights, without adequate instruction and protection. Helmets and protective boots are necessary for pupils working on large constructions.

3.68 Environmental, rustic and rural craftwork often necessitates the use of a wide variety of tools outdoors. Appropriate clothing will sometimes include helmets, gloves and eyeshields. Certain tools such as spades, forks, axes, saws etc must be sheathed when going to and from sites. Power driven equipment must be used only by suitably qualified persons and where there is no risk of distractions. Cooperative working and mutual concern for each other's safety are important elements in such activities, and pupils must be alerted to hazards ranging from the whiplash of a branch of a tree to the unskilled use of a tool (see Chapter 6, particularly paragraphs 6.44 to 6.54).

Motor vehicle work

3.69 When internal combustion engines are operated inside buildings the exhaust fumes must be properly discharged to the open air. Petroleum spirit or mixture must be contained in metal cans which should be kept in an approved store-room[1]. If a supply of petroleum spirit is stored in a school a licence may be required; the petroleum department of the local authority should be consulted. In any area where battery charging or the testing of fuel injection systems is carried out there must be good ventilation and no sources of ignition. Inspection pits are occasionally provided in schools; these often present serious hazards. They should be of adequate length to allow the pupils and the teacher safe access and exit while a car is in position. If there is an inspection pit, petrol may enter it. Since petrol vapour is heavier than air it will remain there and be a hazard if there is any source of ignition. All sources of ignition must therefore be excluded. Exceptionally, electric lighting may be permitted, provided that either all fittings are certified flameproof and the wiring system is suitable or, alternatively, the electric system is continuously purged with air. More details are given in BS 5345[17]. (See also paragraph 3.29.) Special care should be taken when any type of lifting equipment is used. Lifting jacks are for raising vehicles; they should never be used as supports while work is in progress. Jacks must be replaced by adequately rigid supports before any work is begun on the vehicle. Risk of injury while working on running engines, eg adjusting the timing, can arise if the operator touches a high voltage lead and pulls his hand away on to a projection or a revolving part.

Go-karts 3.70 Advice on the construction of go-karts can be obtained from the National Schools Karting Association[18]. Safety helmets and protective clothing should always be worn by pupils when driving go-karts.

Aircraft and boat building

3.71 Only thoroughly tested and proved constructions should be undertaken in schools. Expert advice is necessary before and during the building of an aircraft. (See comments concerning building boats, canoes, powered aircraft and gliders in the DES Safety Series No 1[19].)

Work with plastics

3.72 Work with plastic materials brings additional hazards into school workshops. Many of the materials used (polymers, resins, adhesives and materials acting as catalysts and accelerators) readily produce very dangerous situations in the form of poisonous fumes, skin irritants, risk of fire and explosions. It is very important that the teachers involved are aware of these risks and that they take appropriate precautions as detailed in Appendix 5.

Technology

3.73 Many CDT courses involve technological elements which require specialised equipment to be introduced into the workshop, or certain processes and activities to be combined which might constitute potential hazards. In addition to the relevant points in this pamphlet, DES Safety Series No 2[20], should be carefully studied. Some of the areas of danger associated with this work are described in the following paragraphs.

Pneumatics 3.74 Air under high compression constitutes a potential hazard[1]. The following points are important:
- Air hoses should be inspected frequently for wear, damage or faulty couplings.
- When air hoses under pressure are disconnected at one end they can snake dangerously.
- Teachers should guard against horseplay with pneumatic equipment. Very serious bodily damage can occur if an open air-pipe is directed into an ear, eye, mouth etc. It is advisable to operate pneumatic equipment at the lowest pressure commensurate with working efficiency.
- The use of fixed pressure relief valves on compressors is preferable to the use of adjustable safety valves. The former cannot be screwed down accidentally or deliberately, and therefore safe working pressures cannot be exceeded.
- Mechanisms operated by compressed air, such as cylinder-operated rams, can tap or crush fingers and other parts of the body. The air supply should be cut off whilst adjustments are being made or when decisions are made about the need for guards.
- Home-made pneumatic components should not be used.
- Compressed oxygen cylinders must never be connected to a pneumatic system.
- Air receivers require special care. Where possible they should be installed outside the workshop. Insurance, regular inspection (at least once in two years) and regular cleaning are essential. Drainage plugs must be placed at the lowest point of the receiver, which should be drained daily when in use. The strictest attention should be given to the manufacturers' recommendations for installation, use and maintenance.

Electricity and electronics 3.75 (See also Chapter 3 in DES Safety Series No 2[20], Safety in science laboratories and Appendix 1). As a general principle, permanent mains wiring should not be taught in schools. There will be occasions where technology projects use mains wiring in equipment which is connected to the main supply by plug and socket. No teacher should attempt to teach the principles of such work without a thorough knowledge of and specialised training in electrical wiring. Any work must comply with the regulations issued by the Institution of Electrical Engineers[3]. Useful guidance on such matters appears also in the Schools Council's Project Technology Handbook No 13[21].

3.76   Technology courses often make extensive use of portable electrical equipment (see also paragraphs 3.63 to 3.65). Commercial equipment and school-built kits such as power packs should be tested regularly. The following points are emphasised:

- Earthing. Resistance measurements from all earthed metalwork to earth pin on mains plugs should approximate to zero. Terminals should be checked for grip and signs of corrosion.
- Fuses and leads. Ratings of fuses should be related to the type of equipment. Switches or fuses should always break the live lead, which must be coloured red or brown. New standard PVC sheathed flexible cable should be used and the terminal wiring and the polarity should be checked for correctness. Wiring on old or foreign equipment should be changed, if necessary, to meet present standards[3]. All leads deteriorate in use. It is therefore recommended that periodic checks are made by a qualified person to ensure that insulation standards are maintained.
- Risks associated with tampering. Pupils may, with metal instruments, poke through protective casings or unscrew panels on electrical equipment, and possibly expose live circuits. The replacement of screws by pop-rivets is a useful barrier against tampering, and use should be made of warning signs and notices.
- Pilot lights should be installed wherever possible and checked regularly.
- Physical conditions. Heat produced by some electrical equipment can be a fire hazard. The casing of such equipment should be of non-combustible material. A common danger in electronics work is the risk of burning leads when soldering irons are being used. Cables should be protected by flexible sleeves, and their physical condition should be carefully checked periodically. Teachers must beware of the effects of damp conditions or fuel vapours on electrical equipment. Only equipment designed and tested to operate under such conditions should be used, and any doubts

should be referred to authorised contractors for professional advice.
- First aid. Teachers and pupils should have some knowledge of modern methods of resuscitation and should know how to deal with electric shock.

3.77   Much of electrical and electronics work also involves a wide variety of other crafts and practical activities, and teachers should study all the relevant advice available, and ensure that working conditions, facilities, materials and equipment are suitable.

Flammable liquids and gases   3.78   Technological projects often involve the use of flammable liquids and gases. Relevant Government regulations on the storage and use of flammable liquids/gases must be adhered to. (See paragraph 3.69 and Appendix 2 in this pamphlet and also BS 4163[1].) In addition:
- One particular hazard is the risk of ignition of flammable liquids on school-built go-karts, hovercraft and similar small-engined vehicles and test rigs. Petrol tanks can be filled with substances which minimise the risk of tank explosion. However, the dangers often relate to risks of ignition outside the fuel tank. Dense vapours may flow and accumulate some distance from the point of filling and be ignited by a flame or a spark. There is also a fire risk when using methylated spirits as a fuel for small steam engines.
- Because of flammable gas given off by batteries when on charge, care should be taken to avoid sparking by switching off the power supply before charger leads are connected or disconnected. Battery terminals should be shielded, since a battery contains energy and a spark can be caused by any conductor which touches its terminals or exposed connecting straps.

Departmental interchange   3.79   Technological projects increasingly involve teachers from several school departments. Where there is likely to be interchange of staff between, for example, school workshops and science laboratories, special care must be taken to ensure that teachers are aware of any unfamiliar hazards to themselves and to pupils.

Conclusion

3.80   The discussion of safety precautions and accident prevention should be an important part of any course in the workshop. In the types of course for senior pupils which have been mentioned briefly in this section, these aspects will need particular consideration. Situations may arise which will enable teachers to relate the work to industrial problems. When these occur, one valuable element of the course may be a discussion between pupils and others concerned with safety in school, industry and the wider community.

CDT department checklist

How safe is your workshop?

1. Do you have a copy of BS 4163? This should be read in conjunction with this publication.

2. Do you have a first aid kit in each workshop?
    It should contain an inventory. The contents should be checked regularly. Pupils should know what to do in the case of an accident.

3. Is each workshop provided with suitable fire extinguishers, sand buckets, scoop and fire blankets?
    Pupils should know how and when to use them. Teachers and pupils should be aware of the likely causes of spontaneous combustion. Flammable materials should be stored safely in accordance with Government regulations and local authority requirements[1].

4. Is all mains equipment adequately earthed, and are all portable power tools low voltage or double insulated and approved by the LEA?
    Stop switches, or other stopping devices, should be readily accessible.

5. Are all floors safe to walk or work on?
    Abrasive strips or non-slip mats may be necessary.

6. Are your workshop and store-room tidy, with bench tops and floor clear of unnecessary material; is it an example of an efficient safe workshop; are your bench and desk tidy, well organised and workmanlike?

7. Are all the tools in good condition?

8. Do you have goggles or visors for each machine? Or safety spectacles for each pupil? Do you and your pupils always use them and do you insist on their use?

9. Is there an adequate supply of appropriate protective clothing such as aprons, boots, gloves etc?

10. Do all the machines have adequate guards?
    In particular, if you have a circular saw, the guard, riving knife and push-stick should be always used. It should have a locking switch or other means of preventing unauthorised use. The required notices should be permanently displayed.

11. Are the precautions to be observed when using welding equipment well known?
    (See paragraphs 3.32 to 3.39 and Appendix 2 and BS 4163.) All gas cylinders must be stored away from other heat sources and, if outside, in a properly ventilated store. Everyone's eyes must be protected from electric arc flash.

12. Is the ventilation adequate when using solvents for work in plastics or paint spraying?
    Six to eight air changes per hour are the minimum necessary. You should have respirators for such operations. There should be a copy of 'Safeguards in the school laboratory'[22] available.

13. Are you and the pupils aware of the dangers of inhaling certain solvents and absorbing some solvents through the skin[1]?

14. Are the supply and use of acids and other chemicals strictly controlled? Do you know the dangers? Do the pupils know what to do if eyes are contaminated?
    See paragraphs 3.18 to 3.20 of this pamphlet and BS 4163.

15. Are the right safety attitudes being developed?

16. Is there a good team spirit?
    Willingness to assist others, orderliness,
    responsibility and cleanliness promote safety.

17. Are the pupils encouraged to think for themselves, avoid danger wherever possible and be responsible for others as well as themselves?

18. Are all pupils trained not merely to see but to foresee? In other words, to anticipate consequences?

19. Is there a proper respect for tools, materials and equipment?

20. Are all the adults who use the workshop providing good examples, particularly in dress, behaviour and management?
    Are all who use your workshop sufficiently safety
    conscious?

References

1. BS 4163 *Recommendations for health and safety in workshops of schools and colleges.* British Standards Institute, Sales Department, 101 Pentonville Road, London N1 9ND.

The British Standards Yearbook lists current standards and it should be consulted when a particular item is under consideration.

2. Department of Education. Building Bulletin No. 31 *Secondary school design: workshop crafts.* 1966 HMSO.

3. Institution of Electrical Engineers. *Regulations for electrical installations.* 1981. Institution of Electrical Engineers, Savoy Place, London WC2R 0BL. Popularly referred to as the IEE Wiring Regulations. The 15th edition published in 1981 is intended to supersede the 14th edition in January 1983.

4. BS 5378 *Safety signs and colours.*

5. *Code of practice for reducing the exposure of employed persons to noise.* 1972. HMSO.

6. BS 2092 *Industrial eye-protectors.*

7. Association of Advisers in Craft, Design and Technology, Secretary, Mr F W Elford, London Borough of Hounslow, Civic Centre, Lampton Road, Hounslow TW3 4DN.
The Association has prepared three sets of course elements on safety in the use of heat processes, woodworking machinery and metalworking machinery to enable courses to be arranged that will provide a national minimum standard of safety training for the

protection of teachers using school workshop equipment and machinery. It also produces Safe Condition Survey and Report Forms for recording and reporting inspections of school workshops in respect of heat processes, woodworking machinery and metalworking machinery.

8. BS 1542 *Equipment for eye, face and neck protection against radiation arising during welding and similar operations.*

9. BS 2653 *Protective clothing for welders.*

10. Health and Safety at Work Booklet No. 38. *Electric arc welding.* HMSO.

11. BS 638 *Arc welding power sources, equipment and accessories.*

12. Health and Safety at Work Booklet No. 4 *Safety in the use of abrasive wheels.* HMSO.

13. Health and Safety at Work Booklet No. 20. *Drilling machines: guarding of spindles and attachments.* HMSO.

14. Health and Safety at Work Booklet No. 42 *Guarding of cutters of horizontal milling machines.* HMSO.

15. Health and Safety at Work Booklet No. 41 *Safety in the use of woodworking machines.* HMSO.

16. BS 2769 *Portable electric motor-operated tools.*

17. BS 5345 *Code of practice for the selection, installation and maintenance of electrical apparatus for use in potentially explosive atmospheres (other than mining applications or explosive processing and manufacture).*

18. National Schools Karting Association, Secretary, The John Warner School, Stanstead Road, Hoddesdon, Hertfordshire, EN11 0QF.

19. Department of Education and Science. DES Safety Series No. 1 *Safety in outdoor pursuits.* 1979. HMSO.

20. Department of Education and Science. DES Safety Series No. 2. *Safety in science laboratories.* 1978. HMSO.

21. Schools Council Project Technology Handbook No. 13. *Basic electrical and electronic construction methods.* Heinemann Educational.

22. *Safeguards in the school laboratory.* 1981. Association for Science Education, College Lane, Hatfield, Hertfordshire AL10 9AA.

4 Home economics, dress and textiles

It is important to read Chapter 1 in conjunction with this section, because all its requirements in relation to activities in Home Economics departments are relevant, in addition to the following special needs.

Safety training

4.1   In every home economics department, certain safety rules should be taught as part of pupils' initial basic training. They should include such matters as:
- The need for care and consideration in moving about the home economics area.
- Safe methods of carrying equipment and handling materials.
- Correct ways of lifting and moving heavy or bulky equipment and furniture to avoid strain and injury.
- Suitable clothing, footwear and hairstyles for practical work to reduce the risks of fire, entanglement with machinery and contamination of food.
- The use of cookers and other electrical appliances and machinery.
- Hygienic food handling.
- Fire precautions.

The following sections highlight some of the more important aspects of safety in relation to home economics.

Planning the working area

4.2   As safety depends largely on good design and arrangement of working space, expert advice is needed at an early stage of planning. The area should be designed to permit effective supervision, and provided with good lighting and unimpeded circulation spaces, allowing easy access to all sections of the working area. It is most important to avoid overcrowding, unnecessary protrusions from walls or equipment and any obstacles on the floors. Adequate and well-sited storage space is needed, not only for materials and equipment, but also for pupils' personal possessions, such as bags, baskets, coats, etc which are a serious hazard if left lying about.

4.3   Materials chosen for floors should be resilient, non-slip, resistant to grease and easy to clean; floors must be well maintained and in good repair; windows and ventilators should be accessible and easily controlled without pupils or teachers having to lean across equipment, or stand on work tops and draining boards. If window curtains are fitted, they should be some distance away from cookers and naked flames.

4.4   Main control taps for gas and water and the main electrical supply switch should be within easy reach, and clearly labelled.

Furniture and fittings

4.5   These should be chosen with health and safety education in mind; they should be strongly made and not have sharp edges, protruding legs or doors which open dangerously.

4.6   Working surfaces should be of impermeable and easily cleaned material, without cracks or open joins in which dirt may lodge. The height of furniture and fitments should be selected to avoid unnecessary bending or stretching. If possible, tables, countertops, chairs and stools of different heights should be provided to allow for variations in the size of pupils.

4.7   If high-level storage is unavoidable, then stable and well designed household steps must be provided and used.

Equipment

4.8   In line with developments in industry and the house, the modern home economics department has a wide range of specialised and potentially dangerous equipment which can be used with confidence and safety only if the teacher has expert knowledge and experience of its operation, and the pupils are given sound basic training in correct working methods. Manufacturers' operating instructions should be obtained, and the pupils should read and follow directions for the use of all equipment.

4.9   The installation and positioning of equipment, particularly of cookers, is important and must be considered at an early stage of planning. Consideration should be given to the level of the cooker in relation to working surfaces. Adjacent cupboards and walls may need insulating.

4.10   Equipment, such as electric table mixers, with exposed moving parts should be placed on well lighted, uncongested and firm bases, and should not be used by more than one person at a time.

4.11   The installation of domestic appliances should always be carried out by experts and in accordance with British Standard Codes of Practice.

4.12   Safety should play a large part in the choice of equipment. It should be robust in construction and well designed for its purpose. Regular and efficient maintenance of equipment is essential if it is to remain in a safe condition.

4.13   There are a number of British Standards concerned with the safety of equipment. For example BS 3456 deals with the safety of a wide range of household electrical appliances[1]. Equipment complying with the Standard bears the electrical kitemark of the British Electro-technical Approvals Board (BEAB) for household equipment. BS 1250 deals with the safety of gas-operated domestic appliances[2]. Appliances tested by the Gas Council for compliance with British Standards bear a Gas Council approval label. A British Standard also deals with safety requirements for domestic pressure cookers[3] (BS 1746). The Domestic Solid Fuel Appliance Approval Council tests solid fuel appliances for safety in compliance with BSI Standards and issues an approved list. The Oil Appliance Manufacturers Association issues a special mark of approval for equipment which complies with the stringent British Standard for paraffin heaters BS 3300[4].

Fire prevention and prevention of burns and scalds
(See also Appendix 3)

4.14   As fire is one of the most serious hazards in the home economics department and in the home, it is vitally important to educate pupils in fire prevention and also to teach them what to do in case of fire.

Education for safety   4.15   Safe methods of using equipment and of handling materials should be part of basic training. For example pupils should be taught:
• Not to lean across lighted gas burners or hot electric plates.
• The dangers involved when loose hair, clothes, curtains, oven cloths, etc

come into contact with naked flames or electric hot plates.
- The fire risks involved in gas leaks, defective pilot lights, worn electric leads and unsafe wiring.
- The correct method of lighting burners when they are not automatic.
- The necessary precautions to take when more than one person is using a cooker.
- The safe positioning of pan handles when in use.
- The particular care needed when frying in deep fat. This requires close supervision.

It is useful to have at least one cooker fitted with pan guards to show how the danger of scalding accidents to young children can be reduced. The grave risk of serious burning accidents must be constantly stressed.

Fires and fireguards

4.16 There are statutory regulations governing the provision of well fitting fireguards of approved design to all fires, whether solid fuel, gas, electric or oil burning. Portable heaters should be used with special care in home economics areas and mirrors should never be placed above fires, or near cooking equipment.

Flammability of fabrics and design of clothing

4.17 Wise choice of fabrics and of design of clothing are very important factors in preventing burning accidents and it is essential that pupils should be taught about the flammability of materials.

4.18. Regulations designed to reduce the incidence of burns caused by flammable nightdresses, the Nightdresses (Safety) Regulations 1967 (Sl 839), should be in the possession of every home economics, dress and textiles teacher, who must ensure that no garment is made in school which would contravene these regulations. The Home Office produced a report in 1970 on children's dressing gowns which gives useful advice on safe and dangerous fabrics[5]. More recently, in 1979, the British Standards Institution issued BS 5722[6] which may form the basis of revised Government regulations.

4.19 British Standards BS 3120, BS 3121 and BS 4569 also relate to the flammability of fabrics[7,8,9].

4.20 Substances such as glues and cleaning agents can be fire risks if stored incorrectly. Aerosol cans both full and empty are also potential fire hazards. Explicit instructions for the safe storage of flammable substances and aerosol cans are usually to be found printed on the labels of the containers; these instructions should be strictly followed. Combustible materials such as polystyrene chips should be stored in fireproof containers. Fire risks are reduced by storing minimum amounts of the materials required.

4.21   Rubbish and combustible waste material should not be allowed to accumulate in home economics areas. Quantities of oily rags, such as those used in home decorating and painting work, are potential sources of danger as they may easily ignite.

Fire fighting equipment and fire drills   4.22   Every group using the home economics area should be told about, and be familiar with, the fire drill for the area. Pupils and teachers should know where the fire fighting equipment is kept, how to use it, and what action to take in case of fire.

4.23   Stairways and exit doors must not be obstructed at any time.

Electrical equipment

4.24   For general information about installation, maintenance and testing of equipment, siting of power sockets, earthing of appliances, and safety regulations, see Appendix 1.

4.25   As the home economics area and the home now contain so much fixed and portable electrical equipment, it is essential to educate pupils to handle it safely and to be aware of the danger of improper use.
- Electrical appliances should not be connected to lighting circuits.
- The use of two- or three-way adaptors and extension leads must be avoided.
- Connecting leads must not be allowed to trail where they are liable to damage by impact or abrasion or where pupils may trip over them.
- All mains sockets should be for three-pin plugs. Connections between equipment and the plugs should normally be made with three-core flexible cable of suitable current rating, with an outer covering of thick plastic or tough rubber. The exception is the use of two-core cable for connecting equipment, which complies with BS 415[10] and is BEAB

approved (see 4.13). PVC sheathed flexible cable with an outer braided covering may be used for domestic electric irons.

- Pupils should be taught the correct colour coding of the conductors in main connecting cables, ie

    Brown = Live
    Blue = Neutral
    Green and Yellow = Earth.

- There should be some clear indication, preferably a pilot light, to show when an appliance is switched on. It should be remembered that the filament lamp used for pilot lights is particularly liable to fail.

- Electrical apparatus should never be handled with damp or wet hands or when the user is standing on a wet surface.

- Equipment should be switched off when not in use. Portable equipment should be disconnected from the mains socket, and plugs and leads should be carefully stored to prevent damage.

- Apparatus should be carefully disconnected from the mains before making any adjustment.

- In the case of electric shock, the injured person must be disconnected from the source of supply by switching off the current. If this is not possible, rubber gloves, a dry mackintosh coat or dry woollen materials should be used by the rescuer to protect the hands and a dry mat or coat should be placed underfoot before contact is made (See Appendix 1).

- Home economics teachers and pupils should have some knowledge of modern methods of resuscitation.

4.26   Sewing machines should be used in situ where possible and on a firm base. If it is necessary to transport a machine from one area to another a trolley should be used for the purpose and great care should be exercised, especially when lifting the machine.

4.27   Microwave ovens should be installed only if they have been manufactured to BS 5175[11]; an interlock should be provided to ensure that the oven will not operate when the door is open. Precise instructions for care and cleaning should be clearly displayed near the oven, and these should be followed. Regular maintenance of microwave ovens is essential. Research into leakage of radiation from some appliances is currently being carried out by the National Radiological Protection Board[12]. Until its findings are published, if any damage occurs to the door seal or there is any other doubt about the safety of an oven, contact should be made with the environmental health officer.

Science bays

Science trolleys and experimental areas

4.28   Many home economics departments now include an area in which investigational work is carried out. If these areas are equipped with scientific apparatus and chemical reagents, they should be isolated from food preparation and dress and textiles sections to prevent contamination of food and damage to fabrics. Lockable storage accommodation should be provided for potentially hazardous chemicals. Further reference should be made to paragraph 160(vi) in DES Safety Series No 2[13], and in particular to sections on laboratory design and furniture, electricity, fire, chemical hazards and experiments involving plastics. (See also paragraphs 3.73 to 3.79.)

4.29   Care should be taken in the culture of micro-organisms as the cultures can be contaminated by pathogens. Petri dishes are best sealed with adhesive tape and incinerated or autoclaved after use[13].

Poisons

4.30   Accidental poisoning has become an alarmingly frequent cause of illness, and often of death, among young children and special care must be taken to educate pupils in the proper care and use of dangerous substances.
- Any scheduled poisons which may be used for specific purposes must be properly labelled and kept in suitable containers in locked storage accommodation.
- In addition to the scheduled poisons, various dangerous substances such as cleaning agents, disinfectants, bleaches, and stain removers are to be found in home economics areas. These must always be handled carefully, used in the proper concentrations and kept in appropriate and carefully labelled containers.
- Poisonous substances must never be put into lemonade bottles, food tins, jam jars, etc where they may be mistaken for edible substances.

4.31   Cleaning fluids should be used only according to instructions. They may be dangerous when used in unventilated areas, as certain cleaning fluids and powders give off toxic vapours when mixed together.

4.32   Certain detergents and chemicals can cause skin irritations. Careful rinsing is essential and special precautions may be necessary to protect the hands.

4.33   Printing on textiles using wax and a dye is sometimes carried out in the home economics areas. Where this is done, reference should be made to paragraphs 2.14 and 2.15.

Food hygiene

4.34   In order to avoid contamination of food and the dangers of food poisoning, the following steps should be taken:
- The importance of high standards of personal hygiene should be stressed. Hands should be washed, clean protective clothing should be worn and long hair should be tied back when handling food. *Hygienic food handling,* published by the St John Ambulance Association, is a useful reference booklet[14].
- Hand washing facilities and disposable or cabinet type towels should be provided in food preparation areas.
- Sinks, containers and other equipment used for scientific and experimental work should not be used for food preparation.
- Refrigerators should be regularly checked to see that they maintain a temperature below 5°C (41°F).
- Home freezers are a potential source of danger if not properly managed. Manufacturers' instructions for use and maintenance should be followed, and particular care should be taken to ensure:
  - correct packing of the cabinet.
  - Accurate dating of frozen foods.
  - Maintenance of safe temperature (minus 18°C or 0°F). Frozen food should not be refrozen after thawing and should be used as soon as possible after removal from the freezer.
  - Food should be thawed in a refrigerator whenever possible.

– Where food is cooked from a frozen state, care is needed to ensure that the food is cooked right through.
- Materials for dissection or micro-biological work must never be placed in home economics freezers or refrigerators[13].

Miscellaneous precautions

4.35 Sprays and aerosols, which are becoming increasingly common, should be used with care and according to makers' instructions. Some of the substances used are potentially dangerous if inhaled or used in confined spaces.

4.36 The correct use of pressure cookers and slow cookers should be carefully taught, and work with them should be adequately supervised.

4.37 Animals should not be allowed in home economics areas, where they can be a health hazard and can cause serious accidents.

Young children and old people in home economics rooms

4.38 If young children or old people are invited into home economics rooms, every care must be taken to ensure their safety. At all times they must be adequately supervised by the teacher in charge, assisted by the secondary school pupils. The room must be scrutinised for hazards. If parents or other persons not employed by the local education authority are invited to help teachers in home economics areas, prior approval must be obtained by the head teacher from the local education authority.

Working outside school

4.39 Pupils are sometimes asked to take part in work away from the school premises, for example, when studying shopping or housing or as part of child development courses or community service. Before such work is undertaken teachers should check with the local education authority that such work conforms with the authority's regulations.

Conclusion

4.40   If young people are trained to develop a sense of responsibility for the safety of themselves and others, the toll of unnecessary accidents can be reduced, despite the increasing complexity of equipment and the range of goods and materials which are produced.

Home economics department checklist

How safe are your home economics areas?

Regular checking is essential

Working area

1. Is the working area uncluttered and free from all obstacles to safe movement?
2. Is the floor non-slip and in good condition?
3. Is the furniture of suitable size, height and design for safe use?
4. Are working surfaces impermeable and in good condition?

Equipment

5. Is there safe working space round cookers, washing machines, electric sewing machines, etc?
6. Are operating instructions for all domestic appliances clearly displayed and properly understood?
7. Does only one person at a time use equipment which is powered and/or which has exposed moving parts, eg electric mixers or sewing machines?
8. Is all electrical equipment of the approved type bearing the electrical kitemark of the British Electro-technical Approvals Board (BEAB)?

Fire precautions

9. Have all fire appliances been checked within the last three months?
10. Do all users of the area know where fire appliances are kept and how to use them?
11. Are all doors and fire exits unobstructed?
12. Are the pupils familiar with fire drill?
13. Are all fires suitably guarded?

14. Is deep-frying treated as a potentially dangerous activity?
15. Do pupils understand the danger of using flammable materials for clothing?
16. Are loose clothing, hair, ties, ribbons, etc banned in the home economics area?

Precautions in the use of electricity

17. Is all mains equipment properly earthed?
18. Are all plugs, flexes and leads undamaged and in good condition?
19. Is the department free from all two or three way adaptors and extension leads?
20. Is there an indicator (preferably a pilot light) to show when a piece of apparatus is switched on?

Poisons

21. Are the chemicals and all scheduled poisons in the science bay or trolley:
    Correctly labelled?
    Kept in suitable containers?
    Kept in locked stores?
22. Are all potentially dangerous substances kept in appropriate and clearly labelled containers?
23. Are refrigerators and home freezers operating within the safe temperature ranges?
24. Is food in the freezer correctly packed and accurately labelled?
25. Is the microwave oven regularly serviced?
26. Is long hair tied back and clean protective clothing worn?
27. Is there a washbasin with hot water, soap and nail brush and disposable or cabinet type towel easily accessible to all pupils who are handling food?
Finally, are there any avoidable danger points in the department?

References

1. BS 3456 *Specification for safety of household electrical appliances.* British Standards Institute, Sales Department, 101 Pentonville Road, London N1 9ND.
    The British Standards Yearbook lists current standards and its index should be consulted when a particular item is under consideration.

2. BS 1250 *Domestic appliances burning town gas.*

3. BS 1746 *Specification for domestic pressure cookers*

4. BS 3300 *Kerosine (paraffin) unflued space heaters, cooking and boiling appliances for domestic use.*

5. *Children's dressing gowns. Report by the Home Office Working Party on flammable clothing* 1970.

6. BS 5722 *Specification for flammability performance of fabrics and fabric assemblies used in sleepwear tested by BS 5438.*

7. BS 3120 *Performance requirements of flameproof materials for clothing and other purposes.*

8. BS 3121 *Performance requirements of fabrics described as of low flammability.*

9. BS 4569 *Surface flash in pile fabrics.*

10. BS 415 *Specification for safety requirements for mains-operated electronic and related apparatus for household and similar general use.*

11. BS 5175 *Specification for safety of commercial electrical appliances using microwave energy for heating foodstuffs.*

12. National Radiological Protection Board, Harwell, Didcot, Oxfordshire OX11 0RQ.

13. Department of Education and Science. DES Safety Series No. 2 *Safety in science laboratories.* 1978. HMSO.

14. *Hygienic food handling.* St John Ambulance Brigade, 1 Grosvenor Crescent, London SW1.

5 Music

It is important to read Chapter 1 in conjunction with this section, because many of its requirements are relevant to activities in the music department, in addition to the following special needs.

Safety training

5.1 Music is essentially a practical activity and frequently involves the use of sophisticated equipment. It is important that such equipment is handled carefully and regularly checked with due regard to its inherent safety hazards. Pupils need supervision and advice from teachers and safety rules need to be taught if they are to react responsibly when taking charge of musical instruments, tape recorders, amplifiers, etc.

5.2 Practical music classes are often divided into sub-groups, and occasionally individual pupils are asked to carry out their own assignments, with the result that instruments and portable equipment are dispersed in different parts of the music studio, in store rooms, practice rooms and sometimes circulation spaces and other parts of the school. This dispersal puts a greater responsibility on the teacher who coordinates such work and on every individual pupil taking part in it.

Precautions

5.3 Care should be taken to avoid physical strain or injury to anyone involved in the moving of heavy equipment. Teachers should consider carefully the advisability of involving pupils, taking into account their physical ability and the task to be performed, and whether or not personal supervision is necessary to ensure safety. Where castors are fitted to equipment, such as pianos, it is important that the condition of the castors and the surface of the floor over which it is to be moved are checked beforehand in order to anticipate any likely hazards. The opening and shutting of large lids such as those of grand pianos requires care.

5.4 Floors of storerooms should be kept free of instruments and stands, and shelves and cupboards should be large and strong enough to take bulky and heavy equipment; the latter should be stored at a low level to ensure stability and to facilitate withdrawal and replacement. Stackable and dual-purpose furniture, which is commonly used in music departments, requires careful handling, regular checking and prompt action to rectify faults or to withdraw faulty items, in order to prevent the development of dangerous situations.

Music workshops

5.5 A number of schools offer instrument making as an activity. For secondary pupils temporary access to workshops may have to be arranged, but for middle and primary school pupils this activity may well arise from normal class work and may be carried on in the music space or in general classrooms. It is possible to organise a suitable working space and provide a limited number of hand tools within a general area with confidence, provided that effective attention is given to safety procedures. Good lighting and ample space for working is important. Work benches/tables should be strong and stable, and of differing heights to allow for variations in the size of pupils. The need for correct handling of tools, especially those with sharp edges, must be emphasised, and proper storage for them must be provided. Where electronics are involved, it is likely that low voltage dry batteries will suffice for power packs, and an 'electronics trolley' might be developed to a simple design, so that small components can be suitably and easily stored.

Electrical equipment

5.6 For general information about installation, maintenance and testing of equipment, siting of power sockets, earthing of appliances and safety regulations, see Appendix 1.

5.7 Music departments and the home are now likely to contain electrical musical instruments and electrical equipment. It is therefore essential to educate pupils to handle them safely and to be aware of the dangers of improper use. These dangers are likely to be increased wherever portable equipment is plugged and unplugged frequently, or several pieces of equipment are interconnected, or long trailing leads and multi-adaptors are used, or where amateur-built equipment and young people with insufficient technical expertise are involved.

Points to remember
- Electrical appliances should not be connected to lighting circuits.
- The use of two or more adaptors and extension leads must be avoided.
- Connecting leads must not be allowed to trail where they are liable to damage by impact or abrasion or where pupils may trip over them.
- All mains power sockets should be for three pin plugs. Connections between equipment and the plugs should normally be made with three-core flexible cable of suitable current rating and with an outer covering of thick plastic or tough rubber. The exception is the use of two-core cable for connecting equipment which complies with BS 415[1] and is BEAB approved. Braided cable should not be used for connections to portable equipment.
- Pupils should be taught the colour coding of the conductors in main connecting cables, ie:
    Brown = Live
    Blue = Neutral
    Green and yellow = Earth.
- There should be some clear indication, preferably a pilot light, to show when a piece of equipment is switched on.
- Electrical equipment should never be handled with damp or wet hands or when the user is standing on a wet surface.
- Equipment should be switched off when not in use. Portable equipment should be disconnected from the mains socket and leads should be carefully stored to prevent damage.
- Equipment should be carefully disconnected from the mains before any adjustment is made.
- In cases of electric shock, the injured person must be isolated from the source of supply by switching off the current. If this is not possible, rubber gloves, a dry mackintosh coat or dry woollen materials should be used by the rescuer to protect the hands, and a dry mat or coat should be placed underfoot before contact is made. See Appendix 1.
- Teachers and pupils should have some knowledge of modern methods of resuscitation.

Electrical musical instruments

5.8   Musical instruments such as guitars, electric keyboards and synthesisers are often connected to the mains supply, and to amplifiers by long trailing leads. The instruments are very often used in social areas, particularly in secondary schools. In these areas extra danger exists where people can move freely, when drinks are passed around, and where plugs are in or near serveries with washing-up facilities. In older premises such areas are often inadequately served by spaced plug sockets, and the use of multi-adaptors becomes particularly dangerous.

5.9   In music departments, the production of taped music may involve the use of two or more linked tape-recorders together with oscillators, either amateur-made (in or out of school) or commercially produced. The interconnection of such apparatus and amplified instruments needs special care. Hums produced by earth loops should never be cured by removing the earth connection from the internal circuitry.

5.10   Today nearly all electronic musical instruments and amplifiers are solid state devices. The operating voltage for these is usually well below that of the mains. In all cases there is a power transformer on the input side. The primary coil of this transformer, which is at mains voltage, should be fused with the appropriate type of fuse. For maximum safety the isolating action of the transformer must also be protected. This may be achieved by using a suitably designed transformer or possibly by inserting a fuse or thermal link which will operate in the event of the transformer windings becoming overheated. This would prevent a short circuit developing between the primary and secondary coils and the consequent danger of raising the secondary side to mains voltage.

5.11   A fault in the earthing of a musical instrument or amplifier is another danger point. The 'signal' earth of the electronic circuits may not be the same as the mains earth. Metal cases may not be properly earthed in a continuous manner by interconnecting leads. Thus if an earth fault develops, a metal case could rise to mains potential without apparently upsetting the amplifier, or a guitar or microphone stand could become 'live'. These faults could easily develop in amateur-built equipment, or as the result of a youngster with insufficient technical expertise adding new equipment to his outfit.

5.12 The problem for the musician is thus invariably with earth or transformer failure. Portable instruments constantly being plugged in and unplugged are at serious risk of developing faults in the mains input and leads. For improved safety in schools with guitars and amplifiers and similar instruments, protection is afforded by a residual current device (portable earth leakage circuit breaker). This device goes into the mains socket and the instrument plugs into it. A leakage current of a few milliamps from live or neutral lead to earth would trip the device[1].

Music department checklist

How safe is your music area?

1. Are working areas uncluttered and free from obstacles?
2. Is the floor surface in good condition?
3. Are cupboards, stackable furniture and heavy instruments safely sited?
4. Is the piano safely sited? If it is moved, do the castors have free travel over the floor space?
5. Are all electrical leads, connectors and plugs in good condition and correctly wired?
6. Are all items of electrical equipment safe to use and well maintained?
    They must be properly earthed and fitted with the correct fuses.
7. Are earth leakage circuit breakers being used where appropriate?
8. Are all power sockets in good condition and made for three pin plugs?
9. Have you minimised the use of trailing leads?
10. Have the fire appliances been checked recently?
11. Is the music room door free from obstacles, even during large rehearsal sessions?

References

1. BS 415 *Specification for safety requirements for mains-operated electronic and related apparatus for household and similar general use.* British Standards Institute, Sales Department, 101 Pentonville Road, London N1 9ND.
The British Standards Yearbook lists current standards and its index should be consulted when a particular item is under consideration.

6 Rural science

It is important to read Chapter 1 in conjunction with this chapter, because many of its requirements are relevant to activities in Rural Science departments, in addition to the following special needs.

Care and maintenance of animals in schools

6.1 Laboratories used for teaching biology and rural science present the teacher with a wide range of insidious hazards. The hazards involved in handling living organisms and material of living origin are constantly encountered in the ordinary course of life, since all animals are sources of possible infection. It is nevertheless important that their nature should be known and understood by teachers so that risks in school are minimised.

Legal requirements

6.2 Before starting to keep animals in school it is advisable that teachers should be aware of the legal aspects involved. The Universities Federation for Animal Welfare produces useful guidance in two handbooks on the care and management of farm and laboratory animals[1].

Cruelty to Animals Act 1876. This is the principal Act of Parliament which regulates the use of animals for experiment. There are, however, other Acts which touch on the subject to a greater or less degree, and which can apply to those animals not actually under experiment, eg breeding stock. The Cruelty to Animals Act 1876 regulates the carrying out, on living vertebrate animals, of experiments which may cause pain.

Protection of Animals Act, 1911 contains provisions for the protection of both domestic and captive animals from acts of cruelty and from causing suffering by omission (eg not killing or otherwise treating an animal in pain). Veterinary advice must be taken on the treatment and the humane killing of injured animals, and the killing of poultry.

Destructive Imported Animals Act, 1932 gives the Minister of Agriculture, Fisheries and Food power to prohibit and control the import or keeping of destructive animals that are not native to this country. Orders are at present in force in respect of the import or keeping within Great Britain of coypus, mink, muskrats, grey squirrels and rabbits—other than the European variety.

Protection of Birds Act, 1954 details offences in relation to killing or taking wild birds.

Diseases of Animals Act, 1950. This too should be referred to.

Animals (Cruel Poisons) Act, 1962. This contains provisions prohibiting the killing of animals by means of cruel poisons. It is no defence to claim that the poison was intended to kill pests and that reasonable precautions were taken to exclude access by domestic animals.

The Ministry of Agriculture and Fisheries have recently issued an order banning imported bees which may be carrying the Varrao mite.

Animals in the laboratory

6.3   The Schools Council has issued rules for the care of small livestock in schools[2]. Schools contemplating keeping animals need to give careful thought to what it is that they hope to achieve, in the short and the long term. Animals should be restricted to the species and the numbers to which proper care can be given in school.

6.4   Animals should always be obtained from an accredited source. A list of accredited dealers is available from the Laboratory Animals Centre of the Medical Research Council[3]. Specific pathogen-free animals should not be mixed with domestic animals or pets, or wild animals. No British mammal living under natural conditions should be brought into schools. It must always be remembered that animals can be infected by pathogens from wild animals and also from humans eg, dogs and cats can be infected by mumps and diphtheria virus.

6.5   Great care should be exercised to ensure that animal housing is adequate and safe from intrusion from wild forms, and that stock can be looked after during the school vacations. Food materials should be stored in closed bins. It is not wise for pupils to take SPF (specific pathogen free) animals to their homes, where they may come into contact with domestic and wild animals and cannot then be re-introduced to school. Correct management of animal keeping must be ensured to keep animals in good health, and free from pathogenic micro-organisms. Arrangements should be made for regular inspection, and daily cleaning of the cages, tanks, hutches. If steam sterilisation is not available, a disinfectant solution should be used according to the manufacturers' instructions. Animal faeces and soiled bedding must be promptly removed from animals' cages; any animal waste should be put into plastic bags to prevent contact with the waste-bin, and finally incinerated. Waste disposal is especially important with infected animals and microbiological work, and the provisions of the Deposit of Poisonous Waste Act (1972) should be observed.

6.6   Parasitic material should not be brought into schools.

6.7   Wild birds, budgerigars, and parrots should not be kept in schools, as these are potential carriers of disease.

6.8   When handling animals, excreta, cages and cleaning utensils, or water in which fish or reptiles have been kept, it may be advisable to wear protective rubber gloves. Protective clothing should be worn, particularly when cleaning out animal cages. The hands should be washed thoroughly after such operations.

6.9   It should be clearly recognised that there are risks of disease in the examination of dead specimens of vertebrate animals, birds' nests and owl pellets when brought in from the wild.

6.10   There is a potential hazard in handling any preserved material. Formaldehyde solution is irritating to the nose, throat, eyes and skin. Certain diseases are communicable between animals and man[4].

6.11   The table shows a list of diseases that are transferable to man and are associated with those animals most commonly kept in schools. These should be noted—but if all animals are treated as potentially infectious it is unlikely that anyone will come to great harm.

6.12   The larger forms of livestock present some safety hazards. It is important to know that no person under the age of 16 may enter or work in a yard, pen or stall occupied by a bull, boar, sow with suckling pigs or cow with new born calf; handle sheep dip, or work at a dipping trough during sheep dipping operations. Teachers should keep up to date with the latest regulations and guidance[8].

Diseases associated with animals kept in schools

Budgerigar	Psittacosis, salmonella
Cat	Ringworm, cat scratch fever, bite infections
Dog	Ringworm, bite infections, toxocara
Cattle	Brucellosis, Q fever, ringworm
Fowl	Salmonella, Newcastle disease
Goat	Orf
Guinea-pig	Listeriosis, brucellous pneumonia, lymphocytic choriomeningitis
Mice	Lymphocytic choriomeningitis, ringworm
Pig	Ringworm
Pigeon/Dove	Psittacosis
Rabbits	Pasteurella listeriosis
Rat	Leptospirosis, rat-bite fever, ringworm, bite infections (Weil's disease transmitted by wild rodents)
Sheep	Orf, ringworm
Snake	Salmonella
Terrapin	Salmonella
Tortoise	Salmonella

Most animals carry parasitic worms; some are transferable to man.

Details of some of these diseases are given below:

1. Ringworm
Caused by parasitic fungi, can be transmitted by a number of animals.

2. Leptospirosis
Cattle, horses, sheep, pigs and dogs are susceptible to infection and it is a serious condition in humans. Weil's disease is one well known form of this disease, transmitted by wild rodents. Extreme care must be taken when handling wild rats or mice, or materials contaminated with their urine.

3. Brucellosis
Can be passed via the milk of contaminated cattle, or foetal membranes. All school cattle should be Brucellosis tested and kept in Brucellosis-free conditions.

4. Psittacosis (Ornithosis)
The infection is passed from budgerigars and parrots, and causes influenza-like symptoms and possibly death. Pigeons and doves are very often the contact; they may carry the disease which they excrete in their droppings. Care must be taken where there are outside aviaries.

5. Q-fever (*Coxiella burnetti*)
Gives rise to illnesses resembling food poisoning or influenza and occurs through contact with farm animals, or through drinking "raw" infected milk. Ticks are vectors between animals.

6. Salmonella (*Salmonella typhimurium*)
Affects humans as well as most farm animals and is a water carried organism. It is on the increase in calf populations, and hygiene after calf feeding is most important. Care must also be exercised when disposing of poultry.

7. Orf
Is a virus infection causing pus-like lesions; it attacks sheep, goats, and cattle and can cause a skin problem in humans.

8. Lymphocytic choriomeningitis virus
Can infect man either directly from the faeces and urine of mice and guinea-pigs, or by the inhalation of the dried excreted virus from the dust of the animal cage or animal house. In man, the disease may be subclinical or merely an influenza-like illness which, in a minority of cases, can be followed by meningitis seven to fourteen days later.

9. Newcastle disease
Associated with fowls. May also infect man, but produces only a mild infection characterised by upper respiratory symptoms and conjunctivitis.

10. Also associated with working with animals is Tetanus (lockjaw)
Caused by *Clostridium tetani,* an organism present in most cultivated soils, especially those receiving dressings of farmyard manures. Any pupil receiving a puncture wound or bite should have the part thoroughly cleansed and be considered for referral to a medical practitioner. It is desirable that parents should consider immunisation against tetanus for pupils working for a substantial time on rural science projects.

Sheep   6.13   Full scale dipping techniques with hazardous chemicals are currently compulsory. Particular attention must be paid to the use of chemicals such as organo-phosphorus, and the precautions required by the manufacturers must be observed at all times. Where sheep are kept on school premises, arrangements for sheep dipping should be made off the premises, for the disposal of effluent presents problems and there are restrictions on the involvement of young people in sheep dipping operations. At all times it must be possible to control sheep from outside their unit. When sheep are being moved a shedding gate should be used. The danger of children being butted by sheep must never be disregarded; hornless breeds or dehorned stock should be selected.

Pigs   6.14.   The possibility of pupils being bitten by pigs, which are slow to release their jaws on contact, must not be overlooked. Housing should be so constructed as to prevent any possibility of pigs snapping at fingers or legs. Any teacher in charge of pupils must be aware of the dangers of pigs standing or stepping on feet, and whenever pupils work alongside these animals, they must wear protective footwear. It is inadvisable for pupils to be allowed to feed, clean, or handle pigs, unless a responsible trained adult is in the immediate vicinity. Pigs must always be fed from outside the pigsty. It is essential that all pig housing has good ventilation.

Cattle   6.15   Where cattle are kept on school premises, care should be taken that all bull calves are castrated, and all calves dehorned (unless of a polled variety) by a veterinary surgeon. Strong protective reinforced footwear must be worn by pupils if they work with cattle, and where this occurs there must be a trained adult present. All persons concerned with stock must be aware of the dangers of possible transmission of disease to pupils.

6.16   In general the statutory regulations in force relating to the movement of livestock must be known and observed. Satisfactory approved arrangements for the storage and disposal of manures and effluent must be made and must conform to local Environmental Health regulations. Any accidents associated with livestock keeping must be reported, and scratches, cuts, bites must be treated immediately by a medical practitioner and anti-tetanus injections must be given as prescribed (the latter with parental permission).

6.17   If serious disease is suspected, particularly in vertebrate animals, it is essential that professional veterinary, medical, or other qualified advice be sought. Animals thought to be diseased should be quarantined. Under the Diseases of Animals Act 1950, certain diseases must be notified to the police. These include cattle plague, foot and mouth disease, swine fever and fowlpest, anthrax and brucellosis. No post-mortem examinations should be performed in schools.

6.18   It is advisable for local education authorities and schools to consider the availability of money for any necessary veterinary treatment.

Poultry-keeping   6.19   Prevention of disease is vitally important, and stringent hygiene is vital in daily routine, and in disinfecting between batches of birds. Vaccination of the birds during the rearing period should prevent major diseases. Housing must be disinfected regularly to prevent health problems caused by lice, fleas, mites and parasitic worms.

Hazards from allergens and hypersensitivity

6.20   A wide range of materials can cause allergic sensitisation. Dust from the skin, hair and feather of animals is often allergenic, as are pollen and bee venom. Response to these irritants can be immediate, or in other cases people can become sensitised over a period of time. Symptoms vary and may manifest themselves as dermatitis, asthma, or irritation of the membranes of eyes and/or nose. Some plants cause allergies when handled, particularly primula and pelargonium species, also chrysanthemums, ivy and some members of the *Liliaceae* family. The sap of the giant hogweed, *Heracleum mantegazzianum,* contains a substance which on contact with the skin and in sunlight causes a form of sunburn.

6.21   Certain animal and plant materials can produce skin rashes, eg the hairs of caterpillars and stinging nettles. Susceptible individuals must take special precautions, for example, by wearing protective gloves or using suitable barrier creams.

6.22   Venoms (for example bee, ant and wasp) can be allergenic as well as having immediate or direct effect.

Bee-keeping

6.23   It is essential that a code of safe practice should be enforced in all educational establishments where honey bees are kept to establish and maintain:
- A safe environment in the apiary and in areas adjoining those in which honey bees are kept.
- A safe working routine in which an awareness of safety aspects is taught as part of the practical aspects of bee keeping and which ensures that staff and pupils are aware of the medical routine in case of stings.

Keeping small colonies in observation hives

6.24   Observation hives are normally sited indoors, the bees flying through a small hole in the wall or window. This should preferably be in a north-facing position; otherwise it is essential that the hive be shielded from direct sunlight, which may lead to overheating and dehydration. The hive itself should be firmly fixed to a table or wall, to prevent or minimise movement and vibration. There should be adequate access around the hive to facilitate working on it. The hive should not be sited in a narrow passage or where regular movements of pupils occur.

6.25   The flight hole should not open at ground level on to a path or playground; it should be sited so that bees can fly into a quiet area. If a fine wire mesh fence is erected, 2 metres high, the bees are then forced to fly in and out above head level. The flight hole can be used anywhere at first floor level.

6.26   All feed holes must be sealed with perforated or woven wire screening materials. The observation hive should be charged with honeybees and placed in its permanent position by a competent beekeeper.

6.27   Full sized colonies should be sited away from play areas and generally used paths. They should be faced into a solid fence, wall or hedge, at 2 metres distance so that guard bees at the entrance cannot overlook the surrounding area. It is wise to surround the apiary with a fence. If a conifer hedge eg *Cupressocypans Leylandii* is planted around the fence, it provides cover for the coloniser, and forces the flying bees up into the air away from people.

6.28   The use of full sized colonies and the teaching of the techniques of practical beekeeping should be attempted only when a competent beekeeper is available and present. A quiet strain of honeybee should be acquired and maintained. The hives and equipment should be soundly constructed and in a good well fitting condition. Pupils should not open colonies unless very closely supervised by a qualified member of staff, who should hold at least the Preliminary Examination of the British Beekeepers Association[5].

6.29   Pupils and staff opening colonies and handling bees should be provided with protective clothing:
- A sound beeproof veil
- Bee gloves with gauntlets
- White or light coloured overalls
- A hive tool

Pupils attending a practical class, but not themselves handling, should each be provided with a sound beetight veil.

6.30   A bellows smoker should be provided at each hive being opened, at any one time, adequately charged with smoker fuel, well ignited and with good smoke production. The member of staff in charge of the practical class should be attired in full protective clothing and should have a separate lit smoker available at all times during the lesson. When the honeybee stings, it usually leaves the sting behind in the wound, and as it will still be pumping venom, it should be removed as quickly as possible, using a scraping action so that the sting is not compressed. If schools are keeping bees, the teacher in charge must be experienced and knowledgeable ih first aid.

Common plants with poisonous parts

Common name	Botanical name	Poisonous parts
Garden flowers		
Monkshood	Aconitum napellus	all
Aconite (winter)	Eranthis hyemalis	all
Christmas rose	Helleborus niger	all
Foxglove	Digitalis purpurea	all
Iris (blue flag)	Iris versicolor	all
Larkspur	Delphinium ajacis	foliage and seeds
Lily of the valley	Convallaria majalis	all
Lupin	Lupinus species	all
Narcissus, Daffodil, Jonquil	Narcissus species	bulbs (stem, leaves, flower heads and sap may act as irritants)
Garden vegetables		
Potato	Solanum tuberosum	green sprouting tubers and leaves
Rhubarb	Rheum rhapontium	leaves
Trees and shrubs		
Broom	Cytisus (sarothamnus) scoparius	seeds
Cherry laurel	Prunus laurocerasus	all
Laburnum	Laburnum anagyroides	all
Rhododendron	species: and Azalea	leaves and flowers
Yew	Taxus baccata	seeds
Snowberry	Symphoricarpos rivularis	fruits
Castor oil plant	Ricinus communis	coats of seeds
Hedgerow plants		
Black nightshade	Solanum nigrum	all parts
Deadly nighshade	Atropa bella-donna	all parts
Privet	Ligustrum vulgare	berries

Common name	Botanical name	Poisonous parts
Woodland plants		
Wild arum (Cuckoo pint)	Arum maculatum	all
Mistletoe	Viscum album	fruits
Oak	Quercus	fruit and leaves
Toadstools	Various species	all
House plants		
Dumb cane	Dieffenbachia species	all
Hyacinth	Hyacinthus sp	bulbs
Poinsettia	Euphorbia pulcherrima	leaves and flowers

Hazards from poisonous plants

6.31   Many wild and garden plants have poisonous parts. Some examples of the most common are listed opposite. In addition, many seeds, particularly those bought from agricultural suppliers, may be dressed with poisons used as pesticides or bird repellants and are dangerous if ingested.

Pesticides and insecticides

6.32   Insecticides, fungicides and weedkillers may be found in school laboratories and greenhouses. These can be toxic and it is essential that they are used strictly in accordance with the manufacturers' instructions. Aerosols, vaporisers and smoke cones should be used by staff and with particular care; pupils should not handle these substances. When they are used:

- Spray, mist or vapour should not be inhaled.
- Contact with the eyes, or skin should not be allowed but if contact occurs, the affected area should be washed immediately with plenty of water.
- No one should be exposed to a high concentration nor work in a confined space.
- The substances should not be allowed to contaminate food or drink.

6.33   Protective clothing which fits well and is in good condition should always be used. The most suitable is a boiler suit fitting tightly at the wrists together with rubber gloves. The gloves must be frequently washed and dried. Hands should always be thoroughly washed after using chemicals.

6.34   Pesticides etc. should be stored away from living accommodation, main 'farm' buildings, livestock and fodder. The store should be constructed of non-combustible material and kept locked when not in use. It must be a store to which pupils and other unauthorised persons have no possible access and it should be clearly labelled 'Poison'. Greenhouses and other insecure buildings should not be used to store chemicals. Containers should be carefully stored on easily reached shelving. Plastic containers should not be placed in direct sunlight as they are liable to become brittle when exposed to ultra-violet light.

6.35   Each substance in the store must be kept separate from the others, and the oldest in a consignment used first. If there are any signs of leakage, or if a label is missing, container and contents should be disposed of in accordance with the normal practice for the disposal of unwanted chemicals[6]. Stocks must be regularly checked, and a record must be maintained of the types and quantities of commodities in store and the date of purchase.

6.36   If a person who has been using pesticides becomes ill, a doctor should be called at once. If the doctor cannot attend immediately, the patient should be taken to a casualty hospital as quickly as possible. It is most important that information about the chemical that the patient has been using is given to the doctor and hospital authorities.

6.37   Pupils should not be present during outdoor spraying operations, which should not be carried out during rain or high winds. Care must be taken to reduce drifts, and to avoid water courses. All sprayed areas within the school campus must be well marked with a warning sign. All equipment must be thoroughly washed through and cleaned after use.

6.38   Chemicals for the control of certain pests and fungi must be handled with great care. The chart below shows those most commonly used and gives an indication of the interval required after use before safe harvesting.

Pesticide/insecticide	For control of	Interval before safe harvesting (days)
Benomyl	Fungus diseases	—
Calomel	Cabbage root fly	
	Club root	7
Chlordane	Worms (in lawns)	—
Copper sulphate	Damping-off disease	21
Derris (rotenone)	Aphid (greenfly, blackfly, Rose aphid etc)	1
	Flea beetles	
	Pea and bean weevil	
	Raspberry beetle	
	Red spider	
	Thrips	
Diazinon	Beetles	14
	Carrot fly	
	Chafer grubs	
	Cutworms	
	Earwigs	
	Leaf miner	
	Leather jackets	
	Pea moth	
	Weevils	
	Wireworms	
Dinocap	Powdery mildew	7
Fenitrothion	Caterpillars	14
Malathion	Capsid	14
	Leaf miner	
	Woolly aphid	
Methiocarb	Slugs and snails	7
Pyrethrum	Ants	—
	Aphids (greenfly, blackfly, Rose aphid etc)	
	Leaf hoppers	
	Thrips	
	Whitefly	
Trichlorphon	Pea moth	2

Greenhouses, frames, potting and storage sheds

6.39   The greenhouse should be structurally sound, with all glass securely bedded. It is advisable to use only horticultural grade glass, and not attempt to use 'salvaged' glass of a heavier weight. Sheets of glass should be handled with great care, using industrial gloves. The door to the greenhouse should slide or swing smoothly, so that pushing is not necessary. Paths within the greenhouse should be even and flush, and free from algae, to prevent slipping. Staging within the house must be secure and able to support the weight of pots, filling and any applied water.

6.40   All electrical fittings should be installed by an approved contractor. Free standing and open element heaters should not be used; fan blowers should be firmly fixed to a wall. If any supplementary lighting is required for experimental purposes, a damp proofed socket outlet and plug should be used. If natural gas or solid fuel heating systems are installed, these need annual inspection and overhaul.

Frames   6.41   Large sheets of glass below waist height are a potential danger —translucent plastic sheet is a substitute. Dutch lights should be safely stored to prevent accidents.

Potting and storage shed procedures   6.42   All buildings must be structurally sound. Garden chemicals and flammable liquids should not be stored in these buildings, but in an appropriate store provided solely for this purpose. Electrical soil sterilizers and incubators must be earthed and frequently checked. Hay and straw should not be kept in these sheds, but stored away from all wooden buildings. Tools should be stored on racks so that they are at a height for easy reach by pupils. Sharp edges should be suitably guarded. If animal feeds are stored in these sheds, they should be kept in metal or plastic bins with secure lids. Contents should be noted on the sides, including information on chemical or metallic additives if these are present.

Environmental, rustic and rural crafts

6.43   Much of this work will involve the use of hand held cutting tools and machine tools in school gardens, grounds, woodland and conservation areas in situations which tend to be less formal, precise and secure than those in the specialist workroom. Teachers therefore need to take extra care to see that suitable codes of practice are established, known and understood by the pupils involved, and are strictly adhered to.

Use of hand-held cutting tools

6.44   No pupil under the age of 11 should be allowed to use the range of hand-held woodland cutting tools which includes axes, adzes, saws, and bill hooks. Pupils over the age of 11 should use such tools only after receiving specific instruction about their correct use. Hand-held cutting tools should not be carried to and from the place of work in an unprotected state but should be adequately sheathed. At all times the teacher should ensure that tools of any kind are used properly, and so do not constitute a safety hazard. If these tools are to be raised above shoulder height, safety helmets must be worn.

Use of motorised equipment

6.45   Pupils between the ages of 14 and 16 may use petrol driven cylinder mowers, pedestrian controlled, with fully protected drive mechanism, under close supervision. Cut out stop switches should be fitted at hand point. Responsibility for cleaning, maintaining and refuelling lies with the instructor. Electrically driven/mains operated mowers should on no account be used by this age group. Stout footwear, with good soles, should be worn at all times.

6.46   Rotavators, cultivators, rotary hoes and strimmers should be used for demonstration purposes only and under no circumstances should they be used by this age group.

6.47   Chain saws and tree base trimmers should not be available in schools.

6.48   Pupils over 16 should only be allowed to use power operated machinery if appropriate supervision can be provided by staff fully trained in the use of the equipment. Adequate instruction must be given to pupils on the use of each piece of equipment and *the appropriate level of protective clothing must be worn at all times*. The use of powered cultivators should be restricted to those models with forward-drive only, with good safety factors regarding blade, drive and stability. Powered hedge cutters should not be used by any pupils. Teachers using such equipment in the presence of pupils are advised to be accompanied by a second teacher so that adequate supervision is maintained and no distraction occurs. Powered cutting tools should always be properly sheathed when being moved from one place to another. It is important that all powered equipment is adequately guarded and that all guards are properly in position.

Driving of vehicles   6.49   Attention is drawn to the comprehensive legislation regarding children and agricultural equipment[7]. No pupil under the age of 16 should be allowed to handle a tractor or its accessories. No pupil should ride on tractors, vehicles or other prescribed classes of machines while they are being used in the course of agricultural/horticultural operations or are going to or from such operations. No young person under the age of 13 should drive or ride on tractors or other agricultural implements while they are being towed or propelled. Any person who causes or permits a child to do so is guilty of an offence.

Firelighting   6.50   The positioning, construction and lighting of fires must be strictly supervised. On no account should petrol or paraffin be used to start or assist a fire. Fires must be supervised at all times by at least one person who is familiar with emergency procedure in the event that the fire should spread (see Appendix 3).

Tree-felling   6.51   Teachers should carry out tree felling activities only after successful completion of a training course given by a qualified instructor. No pupil should be allowed to participate. Where felling of trees is undertaken, it is advisable that two members of staff be present, one to participate in practical work and the other to supervise the pupils who must be kept well clear of the possible dropping area, that is a distance of at least two lengths of the tree away. The removal of tree limbs should not be carried out by a person climbing a tree for staff demonstration. Ladders may be used, which should be adequately secured. It is advisable that no pupil should carry out this work. The use of aboricultural ropes and harness is not appropriate for school pupils. Any trees demanding such attention should be dealt with by professional aboriculturalists. It is essential to ensure that all timber to be worked is in a safe condition and not likely to collapse prematurely; if necessary a preliminary survey by a trained professional should be undertaken. If chain saws are demonstrated suitable ear defenders should be worn.

Slab-milling   6.52   Only in exceptional circumstances, with trained staff, should chain saw slab mills be used by schools. They should never be handled by pupils.

Personal safety

6.53   In all activities it is important to remember that any young person must not lift, move or carry a load so heavy as to be likely to cause injury. The safe technique of lifting while avoiding muscular strain should be emphasised and taught within the practical experiments undertaken.

6.54   The teacher should ensure that the clothing and footwear of both himself and his pupils is appropriate to the exercise and will not constitute a safety hazard. No one should be allowed to participate in practical work improperly clad, and suitable safety clothing should be worn when appropriate. Wherever pupils or teachers are at risk from accidental blows to their heads, safety helmets should be worn. Teachers and pupils engaged in the use of sharp-edged tools should wear stout footwear. Rubber boots do not generally afford sufficient protection from a sharp blade. Visors or goggles must be used whenever the teacher considers that there is a risk of damage to eyes from flying chippings, dust or thorns.

6.55   Individuals should not be allowed to work in solitary situations where aid will not be forthcoming in the event of a mishap.

6.56   A comprehensive first aid kit (see Appendix 4) should be carried with working parties at all times, and the teacher in charge should be competent to deal with likely emergencies.

6.57   The school must ensure that all parties are satisfactorily covered by existing insurance policies. If necessary additional temporary insurance cover should be sought, particularly for high risk acitivities, where the use of the 'million-to-one' policy should be considered; the National Association of Field Study Officers[9] will offer advice.

Fieldwork farm visits

6.58   Teachers who take children on visits to farms should make themselves thoroughly aware of the hazards presented by farm buildings, grain pits, silos, machinery, farm animals, agricultural chemicals, slurry pits and lagoons, and of the severe risk of rapid spread of fire in straw and hay.

6.59   The number of pupils in a group should be small enough to permit effective supervision. Precautions should include a preliminary visit by the teacher and instruction of the pupils in advance of the group visit.

Rural science department checklist

How safe is your rural science area?

1. Are safety rules clearly understood by all concerned?

2. Are first aid boxes maintained?
   Pupils should know what to do in case of accident.

3. Is an adequate supply of protective and safety equipment kept and maintained in good condition?
   When it is necessary staff and pupils should use eye protection, steel capped boots and shoes, mask, goggles, boiler suit, gloves for chemical applications.

4. Is there adequate and safe disposal of waste material such as broken glass, surplus chemicals, animal carcases?

5. Is there routine checking of: electrical equipment, gas equipment, all exterior buildings?

6. Are fire hazards reviewed and is fire fighting equipment checked?
   Staff and pupils should know how and when equipment should be used.

7. Are all chemicals dated and recorded as they arrive and poisons shown on stock list?

8. Are all containers of toxic, flammable or corrosive compounds clearly marked to indicate their type and the hazards associated with them?

9. Is the total volume of petrol stored at any one time always less than 14 litres?
   It should be stored in approved metal containers each not holding more than 0.5 litres, and in an approved building.

10. Are staff aware of current regulations and guidance[8] in relation to the notifiable diseases of large livestock?

When such animals are kept on the school premises, approved precautionary measures should be taken at all times.

11. Are recognised procedures used for the disposal of: carcases of dead domestic birds, farm livestock and any livestock kept on the school premises?

12. Is the keeping of wild animals and birds discouraged?

13. Is all livestock housing hygienic?

14. Is all electrical equipment installed and maintained by an authorised competent person?
   Whenever possible, double-insulated equipment should be used.

15. Are mains isolating switch locations known and accessible to appropriate staff?

16. Are leads, plugs and sockets regularly checked?

17. Is all electrical equipment switched off and unplugged if not in use or when adjustments are being made?

18. Are all internal combustion engines stored so as to prevent unauthorised starting or removal?

19. Are all staff aware of regulations relating to use of machinery?

20. Are greenhouses and sheds in a safe condition?

21. Are all tools hung or stored in a safe manner, with cutting edges guarded?

22. Does all large livestock housing maintain animals in a safe, clean and humanitarian way?

23. Are there facilities for moving animals without there being danger to pupils or staff?

24. Is slaughtering carried out off the premises?

25. Are only disease-free stock maintained?

References

1. *Care and management of laboratory animals. Care and management of farm animals.* Universities Federation for Animal Welfare, 8 Hamilton Close, S Mimms, Potters Bar, Hertfordshire.

2. In the Schools Council's series Educational use of living organisms, published by English Universities Press two of the booklets *Small mammals* and *Animal accommodation in schools* are particularly relevant.

3. *Register of accredited breeders and recognised suppliers.* Laboratory Animals Centre, Toxicology Unit, Medical Research Council Laboratories, Woodmansterne Road, Carshalton, Surrey SM5 4EF.

4. World Health Organisation *Technical Report No. 378.* 1967. HMSO.

5. British Beekeepers Association, 55 Chipstead Lane, Riverhead, Sevenoaks, Kent TN13 2AJ.

6. Department of Education and Science. DES Safety Series No. 5 *Safety in further education.* 1976. HMSO.

7. Health and Safety Executive leaflet AS13. *Employment of children and young persons on farms in Great Britain.* Health and Safety Executive, St. Hughes House, Stanley Precinct, Bootle, Merseyside L20 3RA.

8. Ministry of Agriculture Fisheries and Food, 3 Whitehall Place, London SW1A 2HH. Tel: 01–217 3000.
Agricultural Development Advisory Service (ADAS), Great Westminster House, Horseferry Road, London SW1P 2AE. Tel: 01–216 7301.

9. National Association of Field Study Officers, Epping Forest, Conservation Centre, High Beech, Loughton, Essex.

Appendix 1 Precautions in the use of electricity

We live in a world in which electrical appliances have come to form an essential part of life, and the study of electricity properly forms an important part of school science courses. This section is concerned with those precautions which all teachers should exercise in the use of electrical equipment of any kind.

Fatal accidents are fortunately rare, but the conditions from which they may arise are not. School authorities and teachers must reduce these conditions to a minimum and take every opportunity to educate pupils into an awareness of the dangers involved and of the need for continual vigilance and care. The major concern is the danger of electric shock which is always unpleasant, but which can be fatal even with apparently innocuous voltages. About 200 people die each year as a result of electrical accidents: many more suffer severe injuries of which burns are a particularly dreadful example.

The severity of an electric shock is mainly determined by the strength of the current passing through the body and the path it takes. Accidents do happen in which the body provides a direct connection between live conductors, as and when the hand or a tool touches equipment connected to the supply. Much more often the connection is between one live conductor and the earth through the floor, or adjacent metalwork. Metal, water and gas supply pipes, radiators, concrete floors and metal sinks provide ready-made conducting paths of this kind and the disposition of power points and equipment should be such as to minimise the risk of the body forming a link between 'live' equipment and such conductors.

A dangerous current may well be produced by a voltage as low as 50AC or 120DC, or even lower for especially sensitive individuals. Much depends on the nature of the contact with the live and earth conductors. Wetness or moisture at the surfaces (perspiration, for instance) and an increase in the area of contact will lower the resistance and thus increase the current with its attendant dangers.

A sensitive residual current device (often referred to as an earth leakage current breaker unit), of the current balance type, should be used as back-up protection when any portable appliance is used at mains voltage.

Treatment of electric shock The victim must be separated from the source of supply of electric current. If it is not possible to do this by switching off the current, rubber gloves, a dry mackintosh coat or dry woollen material should be used by the rescuer to protect the hands, and a dry mat or coat should be placed underfoot before the person is touched. A doctor or ambulance should be called at once. If no breathing can be detected, a recognised method of resuscitation should be applied immediately, for example mouth-to-mouth breathing. If the pulse cannot be felt, and there is no other evidence of heart action, external heart massage should be applied as well. Efforts should be continued until medical help arrives or natural response occurs.

Installations and equipment Electrical equipment in schools ranges from the fixed permanent installations for lighting, cooking and craft, to the temporary experimental circuits used for teaching purposes, which are referred to in DES Safety Series No 2[1], *Safety in science laboratories.* Within the range are included a wide variety of audio-visual aids and the semi-permanent installations of which illuminated aquaria and lighting equipment set up for a limited period are common examples. Equipment should conform with any relevant British Standard or equivalent specification.

The fixed installations should be designed and approved by a qualified electrical engineer and they must not be extended or modified without reference to the appropriate authority. Compliance with the Electricity Supply Regulations 1936 (S.I. 1937) (which are statutory) and also with the Regulations for the Electrical Equipment of Buildings issued by the Institution of Electrical Engineers should be a condition of contract[2]. Within this category must be included such items as stage-lighting and the heavier power-driven equipment in craft rooms, workshops and home economics departments. If the appliances are in regular use, they should preferably be fixed. Metal parts should be permanently connected to earth and this connection should be regularly and frequently inspected by someone of appropriate technical competence. Domestic electrical equipment must now conform to the standards set out in The Electrical Equipment (Safety) Regulations 1975, (SI 1366) and 1976 (SI 1208). A rapidly increasing amount of portable equipment working from the mains will be met within schools (small power-driven tools, domestic appliances and audio-visual aids, for example). Some of these can be the cause of serious accidents. Thus a firm grip on the metal part of an electric drill will produce the low resistance contact referred to earlier on, and a breakdown of insulation in the equipment would set up the conditions for a serious or even fatal shock if the earth connection were not properly made. Some equipment is double-insulated, however, and designed to be connected safely to the mains supply with two-core cable. BS 2754 gives general guidance on construction of electrical equipment for protection against electric shock[3] and BS 2769 gives particular guidance on portable electric motor-operated tools[4]. BS 5420 gives recommendations as to the protection of persons from contact with 'live' parts and of equipment from ingress of solid bodies and of liquids[5].

Connections and switches

There needs to be constant concern for the safety of the connection between the appliance and the power point. Switches should always break the live lead, which should be coloured red or brown, and in some instances a double pole switch should be used to ensure complete isolation from the supply. There should be some clear indication, preferably a pilot light, when a piece of apparatus is switched on. It should be remembered that filament lamps used in pilot lights, are liable to failure. The external metal parts of any equipment should be earthed. This, if done properly, would ensure that a fault in the apparatus will cause the fuse or circuit breaker to interrupt the supply. Earthing does not, however, make the inside innocuous and before making any adjustment, even replacing a faulty lamp, the apparatus should be completely disconnected from the mains by removal of the mains plug.

Making a good earth connection, testing it and assessing its fitness for the purpose is a part of the general installation, and calls for specialised knowledge and full compliance with the Institution of Electrical Engineers Regulations[2]. All single phase mains power sockets should be for three pin plugs. Connections between equipment and the plugs should normally be made with three-core flexible cable of suitable current rating with an outer covering of thick plastic or tough rubber. The exception is the use of two-core cable for connecting equipment which complies with BS 415[6] and is BEAB approved (see 4.13). Braided cable should not be used for connections to equipment except for domestic electric irons when PVC sheathed flexible cable with an outer braided covering may be used. Unbreakable plugs are preferable to the brittle plastic type since they are less liable to mechanical damage. It should be noted that the colour coding of the conductors in the mains connecting cable fitted to electrical equipment of foreign manufacture does not always conform to the Electrical Appliances Colour Code Regulations 1969 (SI 310)

Brown = Live (L)   Blue = Neutral (N)   Green and yellow = Earth (E)

The safest course is to change the whole connecting cable for one with colours conforming to this code.

Safety devices and precautions   Fuses and circuit breakers are important safety devices and in replacing them care should be taken to use the correct type and rating. It is desirable to keep a stock of suitable spares for this purpose, but the cause of the fuse failure must always be sought before deciding whether to replace the fuse.

Regular and systematic inspections and testing of equipment, connections and earth circuits are necessary. This calls for technical skill and training, and school authorities should ensure that a competent person is assigned to the task. Records of all tests should be kept either in a log book or on an equipment record card. The interval between tests will vary in different schools, but it should never be more than a year and when the equipment is in frequent use, it should be shorter.

Because safety demands it and also because of the need to inculcate sound habits in pupils, the teacher should at all times take the prescribed precautions and whenever dealing with electrical equipment he should demonstrate the need for the greatest care. Electrical appliances should not be connected to the lighting circuit. On each occasion when an appliance is used the cable and plug connections should be examined for wear or displacement, particularly at the point where the cable enters the plug. Old or threadbare cable should never be used. Pilot lights must be working. In the wiring of semi-permanent installations such as aquaria, particular care must be exercised to make them safe so that the mains voltage is never brought to an exposed contact by an extension lead. Unexpected heat in a plug or socket may well indicate a loose connection. These are examples of possible sources of danger. The very rapid extension in the use of electricity multiplies these possibilities enormously and increases the responsibility which teachers have in preparing their pupils for its use.

References

1. Department of Education and Science. DES Safety Series No. 2. *Safety in science laboratories.* 1978. HMSO.

2. Institution of Electrical Engineers. *Regulations for electrical installations.* 1981. Institution of Electrical Engineers, Savoy Place, London WC2R OBL. Popularly known as the IEE Wiring Regulation. The 15th edition, published in 1981, is intended to supersede the 14th edition in January 1983.

3. BS 2754. *Memorandum. Construction of electrical equipment for protection against electric shock.* 1976. British Standards Institute, Sales Department, 101 Pentonville Road, London N1 9ND.

4. BS 2769. *Portable electric motor-operated tools.* 1964.

5. BS 5420. *Specification for degrees of protection of switchgear and controlgear for voltages up to and including 1000 V ac and 1200 V dc.* 1977.

6. BS 415. *Specification for safety requirements for mains-operated electronic and related apparatus for household and similar general use.* 1979.

Appendix 2 Compressed gas cylinders: storing and handling

Cylinder gases may be used in schools for a variety of purposes including the processes of brazing, cutting and welding, and attention is drawn to paragraphs 3.27 to 3.36 of this publication and to BS 4163 which deal with these processes[1].

There are serious hazards associated with the storage and handling of gas cylinders and fittings, and standard precautions should be strictly observed in dealing with them. Rigorous rules of safe practice, based on expert and official recommendations, but taking into account the specific conditions existing in the particular work and storage areas, should be formulated. These rules should cover all foreseeable contingencies to ensure that cylinders are stored in safe conditions, properly maintained and always handled with special care so that constant efforts are made to eliminate the possibilities of leakage, fire and explosion.

The cylinder gases that are used in these processes are oxygen, acetylene and liquid petroleum gas (LPG).

Safety requirements for all three gases are:
Cylinders must be stored in a fire resistant, dry and well ventilated space, away from any source of heat or ignition and protected from ice, snow or direct sunlight.
Valves of cylinders in store must always be kept uppermost and closed, even when the cylinder is empty.
The caretaker must be fully informed and have a key of any store in which cylinders are kept.
The number of cylinders stored should be kept to a minimum.
Cylinders should be handled with care and only by personnel who are reliable, adequately trained and fully aware of all associated hazards.
Damaged or leaking cylinders should be immediately taken outside into the open air, and the supplier should be notified.
No one should approach a gas cylinder store with a naked light or cigarette.

Care should be taken to avoid striking or dropping cylinders, or knocking them together.

Cylinders should never be used as rollers.

One cylinder should never be filled from another.

Every care must be taken to avoid accidental damage to cylinder valves.

Valves must be operated without haste, never fully opened hard against the back stop (so that other users know the valve is open), and never wrenched shut but turned just securely enough to stop the gas.

Before removing or loosening any outlet connections, caps or plugs a check should be made that the valves are closed.

When changing cylinders, close all valves and appliance taps, and extinguish naked flames, including pilot jets, before disconnecting them. When reconnecting, ensure that all connections and washers are clean and in good condition, and do not overtighten them.

Immediately a cylinder becomes empty, close its valve.

A clear policy should be established regarding responsibility when gas cylinders and equipment are used also by youth or adult evening classes under the supervision of a different teacher. This must include the reporting of any faults.

Safety requirements for acetylene:
Cylinders must always be stored and used in the upright position.
If a cylinder becomes heated accidentally or becomes hot because of excessive backfiring, immediately shut the valve, detach the regulator, take the cylinder out of doors well away from the building, immerse it in or continuously spray it with water, open the valve and allow the gas to escape until the cylinder is empty.

Safety requirements for oxygen
No oil or grease should be used on valves or fittings.
Cylinders with convex bases should be used in a stand or held securely to a wall.

Safety requirements for LPG
Cylinders and storerooms should be boldly marked as highly flammable with the appropriate symbol.
The store must be kept free of combustible material, corrosive material and cylinders of oxygen.

Cylinders must not be stored below ground level or near drains, cellars, basement, or any similar confined lower space where leaking gas might accumulate.
The correct type of regulator must be used for the particular gas.
All pipelines, tubing and fittings should be of approved specification, according to the grade of LPG being used.

Reference should be made to the Home Office Code of Practice, *Keeping of LPG in cylinders and similar containers*[2], and to the Highly Flammable Liquids and Liquefied Petroleum Gases Regulation 1972[3].

Expert advice on all procedures involved with all gas cylinders is available from professional, trade and commercial organisations[4].

References

1. BS 4163. *Recommendations for health and safety in workshops of schools and colleges.* British Standards Institute, Sales Department, 101 Pentonville Road, London N1 9ND.
The British Standards Yearbook lists current standards and its index should be consulted when a particular item is under consideration.

2. *Code of practice: keeping of LPG in cylinders and similar containers.* 1973, HMSO.

3. *Highly flammable liquids and liquefied petroleum gases Regulations.* (S.I. No. 917) 1973 HMSO.

4. For example: The Welding Institute, 54 Princes Gate, London SW7 2PG. British Oxygen Company, Brentford, Middlesex TW8 9DG.

Appendix 3 Fire precautions

Fire instructions There should be a fire notice, preferably near the door, in every teaching space. The notice should read FIRE in large letters and should deal with:
- the action to be taken on discovering a fire
- the nature of the fire warning
- the action to be taken when the fire warning is heard

Fire drills Careful consideration needs to be given to the quick evacuation of the building when a fire warning has sounded. Occasional fire drills are necessary to accustom staff and pupils to the correct procedures.

Fire-fighting appliances Fire appliances should be kept inside each workroom as near to the door as possible, but away from any part of the room where the fire risk is greatest. They should be checked annually by experts, and the date of inspection should be noted on the appliance. They should be kept in good order and in a constant state of readiness as recommended in British Standard BS 5306[1].

The following appliances are needed in each workroom:
- A fire blanket in a suitable container fixed to the wall in such a position that there is ample space for the blanket to be readily and easily withdrawn in a downwards direction.
- A bucket of sand with a scoop.
- A suitable number of fire extinguishers, usually of the carbon dioxide type.

Staff and pupils should know how to use the fire appliances.

Fire escapes Fire doors should have appropriate notices and should never be left open. Stairways and escape doors should never be obstructed.

Action in the event of fire If a fire occurs, pupils should be directed to leave the workroom immediately. If possible, windows and doors should be closed, the fire should be attacked with appropriate extinguishers, the fire brigade should be called and any other action taken which is required by the school fire instructions.

Fire prevention   Some likely causes of fire in practical workrooms are:
- ignition of flammable materials in overheated storerooms (see Appendix 5);
- explosive reaction or spontaneous combustion from mixing certain substances which are relatively stable alone (see Appendix 5 and DES Safety Series No 2[2]);
- ignition of escaping gases and vapours (see Appendices 2 and 5);
- electrical sparking due to faulty circuits, switchgear etc, (see Appendix 1);
- ignition of flammable materials due to careless and accidental misdirection of flames from gas burners and torches;
- sun rays focused by bottles etc, on to flammable materials.

It is, therefore, of utmost importance that teachers should:
- know the likely hazards of all materials, equipment and processes that come within their responsibilities;
- establish and operate good safety policies;
- give adequate emphasis to the safety training of pupils;
- insist on a high standard of maintenance within the workroom;
- give a clear lead to all pupils by their own personal example.

References

1. BS 5306 Pt 3 *Portable fire extinguishers*. British Standards Institute, Sales Department, 101 Pentonville Road, London N1 9ND.
The British Standards Yearbook lists current standards and its index should be consulted when a particular item is under consideration.

2. Department of Education and Science. DES Safety Series No. 2. *Safety in science laboratories*. 1978. HMSO.

Appendix 4 First aid

First aid is the immediate and temporary care given until the services of a medical practitioner can be obtained.

First aiders All teachers should have a simple working knowledge of first aid and it is important for them to be able to recognise a situation where medical advice is necessary. It is also desirable that some teachers in every school should have attended a course of training and taken a certificate in first aid issued by the British Red Cross[1] or the St John Ambulance Association[2].

First aid instruction should enable a teacher to be able to:

- separate a person(s) from the source of the hazard, eg live electrical contact;
- prevent any heavy loss of blood;
- maintain breathing and offer resuscitation by modern methods;
- deal with burns, chemical or otherwise;
- prevent shock;
- deal with localised injuries, eg to the eye.

The names of those so qualified should be made known to teachers and pupils in order that in the event of an accident first aid may be given without delay.

The object of first aid is to give help at once to pupils, or staff, who are injured or suddenly taken ill before expert help from a doctor or nurse is available or the ambulance arrives. It is aimed at helping recovery, saving life and preventing the injury from becoming worse. Reassurance of the patient and protection from further danger play an important part.

First aid regulations The first aid regulations which came into effect on 1 July 1982 cover all employees in schools, colleges and polytechnics – teaching and non-teaching staff whether engaged in daytime or evening duties. Although pupils and students are not covered by the regulations, employers – local education authorities, boards of governors or proprietors – have a continuing moral duty to provide for them and any visitors.

The Approved Code of Practice for the Health and Safety Regulations 1981 and guidance note are brought together in *First Aid at Work* (HS(R) 11) published by the Health and Safety Executive and available from HMSO and through booksellers.

Suitably equipped first aid boxes should be located in easily accessible places, together with one in each laboratory, gymnasium/sports hall, workshop and home economics/catering area. In order to avoid any duplication of provision all first aid boxes, whether provided under the regulations for employees or for pupils or students should contain only the following items:

- card giving general first-aid guidance (as set out in First aid at work)
- individually wrapped sterile adhesive dressings
- sterile eye pads, with attachment
- triangular bandages (sterile or, if not, with suitable sterile coverings for serious woulds)
- safety pins
- a selection of medium, large and extra-large sterile unmedicated dressings.

Travelling first aid kits should be available to groups taking part in outside activities. Items included in such kits should be restricted to those contained in the list.

The purpose of restricting the contents of first aid boxes to the above items is that an untrained person can use them, in the absence of a first-aider, without exacerbating the injury and until further help can be obtained if necessary.

Staff responsible for first-aid should check all first aid boxes and remove any items not included in the above list. They should also carry out regular inventories of the contents of all boxes to ensure that adequate supplies of each item are available.

Where a first-aid or medical room is provided it may be equipped with additional items necessary for the treatment and welfare of students and staff but should be available for use only by first-aiders. Guidance on the contents for such rooms may be sought from Medical Advisers and may vary according to the circumstances but should be within the principles laid down in the new regulations.

In colleges and polytechnics consideration should be given to the nature of the undertaking. Research and teaching laboratories and workshops could be classified as areas of high risk. The level of first aid provision should always be commensurate with the hazard.

Teaching first aid   Organisations such as the British Red Cross Society and the St John Ambulance Association[2] have training schemes for young people over the age of 11 years and instruction will be given in schools if requested. Pupils receive instruction which should enable them to recognise whether a particular injury calls for expert attention, and to render such immediate help as will prevent further injury. It is clearly dangerous however, for pupils to be given more advanced training than their age, experience and sense of responsibility warrant. They should understand the dangers involved in trying to move persons who have met with serious accidents or to do anything (except to treat for shock and to send immediately for skilled help) in cases of serious injury.

All teachers and senior pupils should have some knowledge of modern methods of resuscitation so that they can help someone suffering from electric shock or rescued from drowning. Clear instructions should be hung in appropriate places. The sixth edition of *The practical first aid* from the British Red Cross Society[1] contains clear descriptions of modern methods of artificial respiration and first aid for victims of electric shock.

Epilepsy   During a major convulsion with loss of consciousness all that is necessary is, as far as possible, to keep the pupil lying on his side to maintain an airway and prevent suffocation from phlegm etc. This is not easy during convulsive movements, but quite easy when they subside, and it is essential. Next, during the convulsion, it is best not to hold the pupil firmly, but only to so control the pupil that injury from knocking into hard objects such as furniture is minimal. On no account must anything be put into the mouth—least of all the fingers. Side or face down position takes care of dangers from tongue-occlusion, and tongue-biting is rare. If micturition and confusion occur the pupil may need to lie down under observation for a while, but sometimes epileptics recover very quickly. Individual handling according to the person and his pattern of fits is required. Most convulsions are over within a few minutes. A doctor should be called if the convulsions are not over within about 5 minutes. Petit mal needs no first aid.

References

1. British Red Cross Society, 9 Grosvenor Crescent, London SW1X 7EQ.
2. St John Ambulance Association, 1 Grosvenor Crescent, London SW1.
3. The Health and Safety (First Aid) Regulations 1981 (SI 917, HMSO).

A comprehensive booklet *First aid at work* (HS(R)11) containing the Approved Code, guidance note and the complete text of the Regulations has been published by the Health and Safety Executive, 1–13 Chepstow Place, Westbourne Grove, London W2 4TF.

Appendix 5 Safety when using plastics in schools

The increased use of plastics materials in art rooms, laboratories and workshops brings potential hazards arising from manipulation and storage. However, if safe methods of handling and storing are encouraged and practised, much of the range of plastics materials available may be used in schools within acceptable safety limits. To establish these methods it is necessary to be aware of the potential hazards associated with each of the materials that are available.

If there is doubt about the hazards associated with any material it should always be regarded as potentially dangerous. Fumes from it should not be inhaled, contact with the skin should be avoided, and it should be kept away from sources of ignition. Manufacturers' advice regarding the handling and storage of materials should always be followed carefully. Many of the chemicals used have distinctive odours, and it is safe practice never to allow an identifiable odour to build up to a predominating level.

Work with plastics, as with aerosols, paints and sprays, should not begin unless there is adequate ventilation. The ventilation should be sufficient to maintain a supply of fresh air in the work area at all times. It is recommended that six to eight air changes per hour should be the minimum, and this generally requires the installation of extractor fans, usually at floor and at a higher level.

Individuals differ in their susceptibility to some chemicals; indeed children appear to be more prone to certain of these hazards. Serious attention should, therefore, always be given to anyone who complains of headache or nausea, and they should be encouraged and helped to seek fresh air. It is particularly important that pupils who are susceptible to asthma are not exposed to fumes. It should be remembered also that most respirators are designed for adults and may not provide pupils with the necessary face seal.

It is important to stress the value of protective clothing when working with plastics. The need to wear safety spectacles or face visors in any situation where chemicals may be splashed in the eyes, or where there is a risk of dust or small particles entering the eyes, must be emphasised. In situations involving the handling of hot materials, resins or adhesives, the wearing of suitable dry, protective gloves is essential. Open cuts and abrasions must be suitably protected before starting to work with plastics.

Fire and explosion hazards
All plastics materials must be stored in cool and dry conditions (the main stock preferably in an outside, brick-built store away from heat sources, open flames and other sources of ignition). Foamed plastics materials are extremely flammable, and extra care must be taken in storing them. The storage of large quantities of catalysts, resins and cleaning fluids will increase the fire risk, and can also be wasteful because of the limited shelf life of some of these materials. A three-month stock may, in general, be considered to be sufficient, economic and safe.

Catalysts should be stored in containers with vents, placed in separate, cool, dry metal cabinets, away from flammable materials. Catalysts and accelerators should never be mixed directly together as this is likely to produce an explosive reaction. Resins are available which incorporate the accelerator, requiring only the addition of the catalyst, and these should be used in order to remove the risk of such an explosion. It also obviates the need to store accelerators.

Waste material should not be left in the work area, but should be removed and stored outside the building, away from fire risk, inaccessible to pupils, and disposed of in the correct manner as soon as possible. Small quantities of liquid waste can be disposed of by allowing them to evaporate in the open air from metal trays. Surplus catalysed resin should be allowed to harden in shallow trays. Waste cured resin and machine swarf should be put in labelled polyethylene sacks and stored outside for collection by the local authority. Rags which have been used to mop up spillage must be placed in a metal bin outside and burnt as soon as possible. Rags soaked in peroxide solutions (catalysts) must on no account be mixed with other waste materials or rags, or used to mop up miscellaneous materials. Special care should be taken to avoid contaminating clothing with peroxide and to prevent peroxide solutions drying on clothing or skin because of the extreme ease of subsequent ignition and the intense degree of combustion.

Skin hazards   The risk of dermatitis is always present when using resins, especially epoxy and polyurethane resins, and these should be used only under strict control. Good washing facilities nearby are essential so that resin contamination can be washed off at once. Barrier creams to protect exposed areas of skin should always be applied before starting work, even when disposable polyethylene or PVC gloves are used. The use of solvents, such as acetone, to cleanse the skin should be avoided as these may be harmful, and the use of proprietary skin cleansers is advisable. Glacial acetic acid should not be used to bond acrylic materials, as solutions of the two substances cannot be washed from the skin by water and can cause severe delayed blisters.

Although the temperatures involved in plastics moulding and shaping are much lower than those for comparable metal processes, it is dangerous to allow molten plastics to come into contact with the skin, because of their high heat capacity and the fact that they stick and are difficult to remove from the skin.

Heaters for forming plastics must be guarded so as to prevent burns, and should be fitted with thermostatic control. Plastic injection moulding machines must be fully guarded on all sides to prevent any molten plastic spraying the operator or onlookers should a mishap occur.

Eye hazards   When working with plastics the eyes are at risk from dust and waste particles of the material and from splashes of organic liquids. When machining plastics care should be taken to avoid a build up of swarf and goggles or eye shields should always be worn. Organic peroxides which are used as catalysts for curing glass reinforced polyester (GRP) will cause severe damage if they come into contact with the eye. For this reason, the measuring and mixing of the catalyst with the resin should be done by the teacher, wearing suitable eye protection. A standard dispenser which is constructed to prevent squirting of the liquid and which is calibrated to allow accurate measurement should be used for this purpose.

If it is suspected that the eye has been in contact with any catalyst, it should be washed copiously and immediately with plain water or a 2 per cent aqueous solution of sodium bicarbonate. In all cases medical advice should be sought without delay.

Respiratory hazards   The evaporation of solvents and the breakdown of plastics materials when heated both produce harmful vapours, and it is important that concentrations are kept as low as possible. Danger is not always immediately apparent because the inhalation of toxic gases may result in reactions which occur sometimes after the event.

When articles are being produced in GRP, styrene fumes are given off which in small quantities in a well ventilated room are not likely to reach a harmful concentration. With larger mouldings, such as canoe and boat hulls, forced ventilation is necessary. Preferably, work should be carried out in the open air. Solvent evaporation is increased in hot weather and the danger of concentration increases.

Styrene fumes are also generated when expanded polystyrene is cut by means of a hot wire. These fumes may irritate the eyes and cause dizziness, according to the concentration and to personal susceptibility. Children seem to be particularly prone to this hazard, and it is important that ventilation should always be generous, and that the hot wire should operate at an even temperature below red heat to reduce toxic fumes. A battery or an approved isolating low voltage transformer should be used to achieve the correct temperature of the hot wire.

When using expanded polystyrene patterns for casting purposes, good venting of the mould is essential in order to minimise the risk of gas accumulation.

The two basic ingredients of polyurethane foam are toxic and should be mixed only by the teacher; the process should be carried out only in the open air. Compositions based on toluene di-isocyanate (TDI) should never be used in schools.

The use of solvents such as petrol, ethanol, ethers and ketones for degreasing is dangerous because they are highly toxic as well as highly flammable. Carbon tetrachloride is not flammable but has a highly toxic vapour and is absorbed through the skin. It should never be used in school workshops. The appropriate detergents are suitable degreasers but protective gloves must be worn.

Machining and abrading plastics

Adequate ventilation and the wearing of disposable masks as well as goggles are essential when machining or abrading plastics. Hand rather than machine methods of abrading are safer, and the use of water as a lubricant cuts down the production of dust. Whenever possible GRP work should be trimmed in the 'green' stage to reduce dust.

Index

The checklists are not indexed; nor has any attempt been made to index items which are immediately accessible from the contents list.